When Your Chronic Illness Becomes a Goliath

Becomes a Goliath

Tami Treat-Boyne

ISBN 979-8-88943-615-7 (paperback)
ISBN 979-8-88943-616-4 (digital)

Christian Faith Publishing
832 Park Avenue
Meadville, PA 16335
www.christianfaithpublishing.com

Printed in the United States of America

Lovingly dedicated to my Savior and Redeemer

CONTENTS

Acknowledgments ix

The Romans Road to Salvation xi

Section 1 Finding a Slingshot to Bring Down the Giant 1

Day 1 It's My Party, I'll Cry *Jeremiah 29 (NKJV)* 3
If I Want To (Part 1)

Day 2 It's My Party, I'll Cry *Jeremiah 29:11 (NKJV)* 5
If I Want To (Part 2)

Day 3 A Time to Weep *Ecclesiastes 3:4–5 (NKJV)* 7

Day 4 Trust and Healing *Proverbs 3:5–6 (NKJV)* 9

Day 5 To Sleep or Not to Sleep *Psalm 127:2 (NKJV)* 11

Day 6 God's Guidance *Jeremiah 30:15a (NKJV)* 13
through the Valleys

Day 7 Your Mission *Proverbs 4:20–23 (NKJV)* 15

Day 8 Called to Prayer *Luke 18:1 (NKJV)* 17

Day 9 "In" Sight *Job 14:22 (NASB, 1995)* 19

Day 10 A Classic Whiner *Jonah 4:4 (NKJV)* 21

Day 11 Barbed-Wire Barrier and *Proverbs 22:24 (NIV)* 23
Hot-Tempered Man

Day 12 Sick and Tired of *Psalm 19:107 (NASB, 1995)* 25
Being Sick and Tired

Day 13 A Cocoon *Jeremiah 10:19 (NKJV)* 28

Day 14 Feasting on the Good *Proverbs 15:15 (NCV)* 30

Day 15 To Endure All *Proverbs 18:14 (NCV)* 32

Day 16 How Serious? *1 Kings 17:17b (NKJV)* 34

Day 17 Endurance *Jeremiah 10:19 (HCSB)* 36

Day 18 Abide with Trust *John 8:31–32 (MSG)* 38

Day 19 The Potter and the Clay *Isaiah 64 8b, c (NKJV)* 40

Day 20 Fighting Your Goliath *1 Samuel 17:49, 50a, b (NKJV)* 42

Section 2 Remembering that God is on Your Side   45

Day 21	Restoration	*Isaiah 40:29* (NKJV)	47
Day 22	Strength	*Philippians 4:13* (NKJV)	49
Day 23	The Good News	*Luke 5:15* (NIV)	51
Day 24	When the World Collapsed	*2 Timothy 3:1* (NIV)	53
Day 25	Bird Doo in Your Life	*Matthew 6:26* (NKJV)	55
Day 26	He Was Wounded for Our Sins	*Isaiah 41:13* (NKJV)	57
Day 27	Be of Good Courage	*Joshua 1:9* (NKJV)	60
Day 28	Hand-Holding	*Isaiah 41:13* (NKJV)	62
Day 29	His Way Is Perfect	*2 Samuel 22:33* (NKJV)	64
Day 30	Make Strong the Brick	*Nahum 3:14* (NKJV)	66
Day 31	My Yoke Is Easy	*Matthew 11:30* (NKJV)	68
Day 32	I Am with You	*Exodus 33:14* (NKJV)	70
Day 33	No Excuses	*1 Chronicles 14:2b* (NKJV)	72
Day 34	Sweet Peace	*Numbers 6:26* (NKJV)	74
Day 35	I Know My Master	*1 Chronicles 16:27* (NIV)	76
Day 36	There's a Fly in My Salad!	*Philippians 2:5* (NIV)	78
Day 37	One Body	*Colossians 3:15* (NKJV)	80
Day 38	Railroad Tracks of Time	*2 Corinthians 1:20* (NKJV)	82
Day 39	Your Burning Bush Moment	*Exodus 3:2–5* (NIV)	84
Day 40	True Peace in God	*Revelation 21:4* (NKJV)	86

Section 3 Keeping a Stone in Your Pocket   89

Day 41	Slingshots and Stones	*1 Samuel 17:40* (NKJV)	91
Day 42	Your Season of Choice	*Genesis 1:14* (NKJV)	93
Day 43	Delight Always	*Philippians 4:4* (NKJV)	95
Day 44	A Look in the Mirror	*Psalm 19:14* (NKJV)	97
Day 45	Fill Me Up, Lord	*John 4:13–14* (NKJV)	99
Day 46	My Strength and My Song	*Psalm 28:7* (NKJV)	101
Day 47	Footprints of the Savior	*Habakkuk 3:19* (NKJV)	103
Day 48	Two Steps Backward	*John 11:35* (NKJV)	105
Day 49	A Vessel of Use	*1 Peter 5:10* (NKJV)	107
Day 50	A Lifeline	*1 Thessalonians 5:17* (KJV)	109

Day 51   New Adventures,   *Psalm 31:24* (NKJV)   111
         New Challenges
Day 52   New Healings   *John 14:2* (NKJV)   113
Day 53   Sufficient Grace   *2 Corinthians 12:9* (NKJV)   115
Day 54   Faith in Our Wings   *Isaiah 40:31* (NKJV)   117
Day 55   Be Still   *Psalm 49:10a* (NKJV)   119
Day 56   The Comfort of Old   *Habakkuk 3:18* (NKJV)   121
Day 57   The Hidden Losses   *1 Thessalonians 5:16–18* (NKJV) 123
Day 58   Wind and Wings   *Psalm 63:7* (NKJV)   126
Day 59   Clay Vessels   *2 Corinthians 4:7* (NKJV)   128
Day 60   Rejoicing   *Matthew 2:10* (NKJV)   130

ACKNOWLEDGMENTS

THANK YOU TO my husband, Daniel Boyne, for believing in me and supporting me every step of the way.

Thank you to my mom, Lee, my daughters, and other members of my family, too numerous to mention, for their support and encouragement along my path of completing this work of my heart.

To my editing team—Leslie, Shirley, and Angella—for their wonderful support and excellent work.

THE ROMANS ROAD TO SALVATION

As it is written, there is none righteous, not even one. Rom. 3:10 (NASB 1995)

For all have sinned and fall short of the glory of God. Rom. 3:23 (NASB 1995)

But God demonstrates His own love toward us in that while we were still sinners, Christ died for us. Rom. 5:8 (NASB 1995)

For the wages of sin is death, but the gracious gift of God is eternal life in Christ Jesus our Lord. Rom. 6:23 (NASB 1995)

If you confess with your mouth Jesus *as* Lord, and believe in your heart that God raised Him from the dead, you will be saved; for with the heart a person believes, resulting in righteousness, and with the mouth he confesses, resulting in salvation. Rom. 10:9–10 (NASB 1995)

Behold, I stand at the door and knock; if anyone hears My voice and opens the door, I will come in to him, and will dine with him, and he with Me. Rev. 3:20 (NASB 1995)

All verses used in the work are NKJV (New King James Version) unless otherwise noted. Other versions used are NCV (New Century Version), the original KJV (King James Version), NIV (New International Version), the Message Bible (MSG), and the 1995 edition of the New American Standard Bible (noted as NASB 1995).

The verses used within this devotional were verified through BibleGateway.com (https://www.biblegateway.com/).

SECTION 1

Finding a Slingshot to Bring Down the Giant

DAY 1

It's My Party, I'll Cry If I Want To (Part 1)

For I know the thoughts that I think toward you, says the Lord, thoughts of peace and not of evil, to give you a future and a hope.

—Jeremiah 29:11 (NKJV)

FOR THOSE OF us with a chronic illness and the plethora of other hidden diseases that go along with each of these individual diseases, the day-to-day life can leave one exhausted emotionally, mentally, physically, and spiritually.

We find ourselves looking for answers to the questions, yet they never seem to come. Answers to things like "What caused my illness?" "When will my pain end?" "How come I can't do what I used to do?" "Am I a burden to my spouse/family?" And the big one is, "When will God heal me?"

We find ourselves losing control and becoming an emotional wreck more often than not. We may try to hide it, but there are times when we just cannot. Everyone knows we have been weeping and crying when our eyes are red rimmed. Our appetite may come and go, or it may come and stay. And the weight just piles on, adding to the emotional wreck of our life.

We think NO ONE understands us, NO ONE listens to us, and for sure, NO ONE can understand the pain and feelings we are having. We may experience a feeling of bumblebees inside our body or buzzing legs. No X-ray or blood test will be able to show what is going on, and it will drive you crazy. Doctors will struggle to determine the correct diagnosis. Maybe you have a disease that was diagnosed easily, but it is developing into more of an illness than you imaged it would be. This, my dear friend, is a chronic illness, and you are the only one at your pity party.

When the air makes your body hurt, and you just do not think you can hang on, rely on God. Stand firm in His grace. He is sufficient for all. Take a moment, and write down where you are hurting today, and let God take it. Practice the art of letting go and letting God. He can carry your burdens. Yes, this may be your party, and you may want to cry, but your illness did not come to stay. It did not come to take away your joy. You will have your good days and your bad days.

(Write down where you are hurting today.)

On a good day, you may be all dressed up and ready to go when suddenly your itty-bitty energy cells shut off, and wham, you hit a brick wall. Pray that you will have the strength to hold on to the Great Physician. He will take away your tears and sustain you. Healing? It may be in your future. Only God knows. Blessings and gentle hugs today, dear friend.

DAY 2

It's My Party, I'll Cry If I Want To (Part 2)

For I know the thoughts that I think toward you, says the Lord, thoughts of peace and not of evil, to give you a future and a hope.

—Jeremiah 29:11 (NKJV)

I WAS DIAGNOSED with fibromyalgia, restless leg syndrome, chronic pain, chronic fatigue, migraines, plus six or eight other diseases over twenty years ago. My doctor had written in my medical chart, "Tends to burn the candle at both ends and in the middle." I was a go-getter to say the least, working full-time, volunteering at church in several positions, and staying busy with family. I had to start saying no to almost everything. Needless to say, that resulting first year brought on major depression and tears. It was my party, and I was going to enjoy it to its fullest. Unfortunately, no one else came. I also did not feel I had a hope and a future.

My boss "encouraged" me to apply for disability. I was no longer wanted at work. I was not asked to help at church. My doctor likewise deeply encouraged me to apply for disability when I asked him. So I began the long-drawn-out process.

Added to all of this, my middle daughter was in a fight for her life with brain cancer. She lost her battle after almost four tireless years of treatments. My party was dark and lonely, and I loved being there. But my family wouldn't let me stay.

Are you stuck in a pity party? No one wants to come to this party with you. No one wants to be with you at the reception table. So suck it up, buttercup, and move on. You can develop all the physical lifestyle changes you want, but healing will take time. Find time with God. He will direct your heart, your soul, and your mind. When those are in tune, your physical health will turn around. Satan will try to distract you from where you are going. Keep your eyes on God, and seek your hope.

When you were diagnosed, what else were you experiencing? When was all this going on? How have you changed since then? (List below.)

Are you being distracted, or are you able to carry on? (Write down your answer below.)

Fill your prayer basket, and lay it at the feet of God. Turn around, and walk away. Do not pick that basket up! Yes, I know this is hard to do. I have been there, and together, today, we will walk away. Pray. Ask God to direct your hope and future. Blessings and gentle hugs today, dear friend.

A Time to Weep

A time to weep, And a time to laugh; A time to mourn; And a
time to dance; A time to cast away stones, And a time to gather
stones; A time to embrace, And a time to refrain from embracing.

—Ecclesiastes 3:4–5 (NKJV)

As you have begun to identify the aches and pains, you have the
weeping and tears. This is normal. Accept it…for a time. But please
do not wallow in it. Do not stay in this place. This needs to be a short
time, just a time of adjustment into a new life. Your new life can still
be exciting, just different. Stop picking up stones of the past. Your
bag will get too heavy to drag around behind you, and you will not
be able to move forward. If you are a type A person, you must find
the freedom to say no.

I once had a church secretary ask me if I knew what the letters
N and O spelled, and I replied "on!" She stated, "I knew you couldn't
spell!" At this church, I was the worship director, ladies' Bible study
teacher, VBS director, children's music leader, fill-in Sunday school
teacher in the children's department and for senior ladies. This was all
volunteer, as I worked full-time at a paid position for a state agency.
Type A? Yep!

You need to take this time to understand what you have and
learn to cope with it. However you learn (books, video, etc.), discover all you can. I wanted to know how my disease (fibromyalgia)
would affect my body. I wanted to investigate the history of it, delve
into the recesses of the past, and discover all that I could, as if I

was an archaeologist, unearthing a new find hidden deep within the earth's crust. This helped me understand my aliment and what was happening to me. I was surprised when I discovered that the 1800s had the first medical literature documented with fibromyalgia information. In 1972, the tender points were described and acknowledged by the medical community as a diagnostic tool for fibro. In 1990, the American College of Rheumatology began discerning new ways to diagnose fibromyalgia and how to treat it. In 2008, fibromyalgia was named a disease instead of a syndrome. Since then, not just one but three medications have been marketed for fibro. There are also other medications that can help keep fibro in check. Put on your safari hat, and dig into your disease or illness to see what you can find out.

By learning about your disease, you will discover a time to weep and a time to laugh, a time to mourn the loss of your freedoms, but also a time to dance about the new freedoms you have with your illness. Remember to find time to embrace your family and your relationship with God. Work on your mental well-being and your physical life. You will uncover on your archaeological dig that you have discovered a map to your new life, and that includes not having to say yes all the time. Remember, you need your rest!

Pray, believing that you will have the faith to fully trust in Him to sustain you during this time. Pray, believing He will not forsake you while He is helping you embrace the new you and your new future. You will not be disappointed! Blessings and gentle hugs today, dear friend.

Trust and Healing

Trust in the Lord with all your heart, And lean
not on your own understanding; In all your ways
acknowledge Him, and He shall direct your paths.

—Proverbs 3:5–6 (NKJV)

WE ARE CALLED to both trust and obey, but there are times in this life that this is very difficult. It is during these times that we are too busy leaning on our own understanding. *Webster's Dictionary* explains the verb *lean* as "to incline, deviate, or bend from a vertical position." How do we do this? Even when we are in the best of health, we can be bent in different ways. We have to look at the reality in front of us and accept it. Occasionally, we need to stop looking in the rearview mirror, remembering what was, and keep moving forward.

We have a choice of two paths; they both have bumps, ridges, and stumps in them. We can take the path to the right that is narrow and high, or we can take the wider path to the left that is low and often not the life that we would wish to live. We will lose God's help and guidance and be bound by negative thoughts if we take this lower path. The narrow path, the higher plain—this one might be filled with bumps, ridges, and stumps; valleys, hills, and waterfalls. But we also have the help of God on this narrow road. He is there to guide us, direct us, and be our helper.

There is an additional part to this verse that I discovered when I went through a horrendous opioid withdrawal. I was hospitalized for almost two weeks, and this set of verses became my stronghold. Add to the above:

> Do not be wise in your own eyes; Fear the Lord and depart from evil. It will be **health to your flesh, and strength to your bones**.

> —Proverbs 3:7–8 (NKJV) (Bold mine for emphasis.)

Since then, this passage has been one of my mainstays. I use it during times of surgery and the refusal of narcotics or the very, very limited use of them so I will not become addicted again. I want to follow the narrow path the Lord wants me on, and for me, that means I want to flee the use of narcotic medications. This is something each of us must discover for ourselves. For you, they may be a medical necessity. For me, they are a liability.

Let the Lord lead you. Let Him find a way to heal your bones. Yes, you may still have your chronic illness. Yes, you may still have pain, trials, and troubles. You may feel the weather changes coming. You may still have your good days and bad days. But you will have the Lord on your side. He, and He alone, is health to your flesh and strength to your bones.

Pray that you will be able to be wise enough to lean on Him and not yourself. Pray that you will be able to find the path that is covered by the Lord as He guides you through the days of learning, growing, and healing in whatever way He wants to heal you. Healing may not mean that your chronic illness will disappear, but it could mean a healing due to therapies and medications. Blessings and gentle hugs to you today, dear friend.

To Sleep or Not to Sleep

It is vain for you to rise up early, To sit up late, To eat the bread of sorrows; For so He gives His beloved sleep.

—Psalm 127:2 (NKJV)

THOSE OF US with any chronic illness discover early on that we keep a different biological sleep clock than the rest of the world. Shoot, we keep a different clock than our own household! They are up, and we are down. They are going to bed, and we are ready to party all night. If we are the early birds, we may live in a household of night owls. And of course, night owls are living with the early birds. There are those of us that are part of the swing shift, otherwise known as a petrified pigeon. We have sleep patterns that are all over the place. We struggle trying to get a good night's sleep using any excuse, such as the phases of the moon, the barometric pressure, tidal waves, wind currents, storms anywhere within a three-day cycle. But in reality, you name it, it can affect our sleep. Many feel that if we could get in a good six hours, we might reach some solid gold in our rest and sleep!

If you don't, what can you do? Lay your burdens at the feet of Jesus. Do we trust Him to take care of our burdens? How often do we place our burdens at the feet of Jesus, just to turn around and pick them up again? If we do this, we are the ones dragging around our own junk, like they have been handcuffed to us. Don't we have enough junk without picking the burdens back up again after we have given them to Jesus? I don't know about you, but my suitcase is full, and dragging around a suitcase full of rocks naming my burdens is not my idea of fun. My junk drawer is full. My trash is full. I need to leave my burdens at the feet of my Savior. Can you afford to drag around a suitcase? Fill a trash can? I watched as a granddaughter pushed our trash can around the house deck. She pushed it off and on all day for three days. What, that doesn't sound like fun to you? To her, it was like she was pushing a go-cart. She took great delight in it. Can you take delight in pushing your trash around? Do you have a spare junk drawer in your house to fill? Who are you gonna call on for help about your trash, junk, or heavy suitcase? There is only One that answers 24-7—Jesus.

Do not fight sleep; your body needs it. If you have an afternoon slump, hit the sack. If you are the early bird, enjoy the sunrise with your Bible, and welcome the new day. If you are a petrified pigeon, take naps when you need them. Get vitamin supplements if needed, and eat healthy. Find time with Jesus whenever you are most awake and aware. If you are the night owl, spend time with Jesus, and take comfort that He never sleeps. To help you find your way, be sure your diet is a healthy one. Caffeine and aspartame are both items that affect our bodies and sleep patterns, as does MSG. Keep a food journal for one month to determine when something wrecks your sleep or gives you good shut-eye. Try to get your vitamins and minerals from foods as much as possible instead of from supplements. You are His beloved, and He desires that you sleep.

Pray that you will learn to rest when you need to. Pray that God will help you listen to your body. Pray that you will become able to sleep peacefully. Pray that others you know that are in constant pain will have healing and restorative sleep today. Blessings and gentle hugs to you, dear friend.

DAY 6

God's Guidance through the Valleys

Why do you cry about your affliction? Your sorrow is incurable.

—Jeremiah 30:15a (NKJV)

WE WILL ALWAYS have both good days and bad days. We will always have days that we do not feel terrific, and we think no one cares. I mean, after all, how can they understand what we are going through? Feeling like we have the flu 24-7? Feeling like our guts are going to spill out? Feeling like our feet are on fire? We do at least expect our doctors to understand. Family sometimes is not much better, and we are left feeling all alone. Okay, okay, I know. You are not ready to laugh all day. You cannot smile. You know, smile "just because." And engaging in an activity that you once enjoyed? Forget it! When you are in the valley, you will feel overwhelmed and shadowed in darkness and suffering. Valleys tend to only have one way out and many times trap you in a cul-de-sac. Fighting your way out of the valley to reach the mountaintop—that's not up to you. That is God's job.

Be sure to talk on the phone to those individuals that will encourage you. Find a hobby that you can engage in that will bring happiness and joy to your life. Take a warm bath if the cause of your sorrow is body aches and pain. Pop in a favorite movie or DVD; grab a beverage, your blankie; and sit back and relax. The more you want to cry, the more you want to be alone and will oftentimes end up alone. Some tears are cleansing. But remember, no one wants to come to a pity party.

Once you determine the cause for your burden, you can work on bringing your sorrow under control and look forward to the happiness that surrounds each of us in this glorious world. Pray that you find a way to walk through this valley. Pray that you will see the beauty through the ashes of your pain and tears. Blessings and gentle hugs, dear friend.

DAY 7

Your Mission

My son, give attention to my words; incline your ear to my
sayings. Do not let them depart from your eyes; keep them
in the midst of your heart, For they are life to those who
find them, and health to all their flesh. Keep your heart
with all diligence, For out of it spring the issues of life.

—Proverbs 4:20–23 (NKJV)

How MANY OF you have seen the old TV show or any of the Tom
Cruise movies *Mission: Impossible*? You are now part of "mission possible." You may not realize how many people are watching you to see
how you are dealing with your chronic illness, but you are on the
frontlines of the battlefields now. And your commander in chief has
called you to arms for this battlefront.

Your mission, should you choose to accept it, is to stand
strong and incline your ear to the sayings of your chief, which is the
Heavenly Father. Your battle plan is to keep His will in the middle
of your heart, for it will be life to you and health to your flesh. By
keeping this, you will suffer less from your illness. Do you believe
this, dear friend? I pray that you do. Your witness will be stronger.

This does not mean that you will find healing. God may answer
yes to that. But it does mean that you will find a way to survive, that
you will learn to rest when you need to, that you will learn to block
negative responses from family, friends, and coworkers—basically,
anyone who does not understand what your illness is and does not
want to learn about it. You see, they have no idea what we are going

through. Some will listen closely. Some will know because they have studied about it. Others will act like they know nothing, as if trying to catch us in some act of weakness. Then there will be those that will seem to know what we have, yet they know nothing about our chronic illness, and they do not want to learn about it.

Do not be a stumbling block to others. Do not force the issue. Pray that you will be on mission, even when your illness is wearing you down day by day. Pray that you will find peace on the battlefield. Blessings and gentle hugs, dear friend.

DAY 8

Called to Prayer

Then He spoke a parable to them, that men
always ought to pray and not lose heart.

—Luke 18:1 (NKJV)

I FIND MYSELF writing this on a day when I have lost heart. Is God not good? He always knows how best to speak to us. He knows when and where we are weak. He knows where our pains are. When we have a night that has been filled with interruptions, leaving us sleep-deprived and facing a day with depleted energy cells, He knows. When we are facing a day in which we can barely walk, move, or sit, He knows. When our hands will not work and our back is on fire, He knows. We must pray and not lose heart.

So find your favorite comfy clothes, something that does not rub or bind. Get your blankie. Grab a favorite beverage, and turn on the DVD. Or light some candles, and take a nice long bath with warm water to help those joints. Talk to a friend, and share some laughs.

You might be facing a storm in your life right now and need to take a moment to just rest and pray. It might come during an actual earthly storm, and you are in a fight for your life. During those times, some things are impossible to do, but you can still pray, and God will fight to help you through your struggles and for your illness no matter what.

We cannot figure things out all the time, but that is okay. Sometimes we cannot even figure out why we feel so bad. We just know that we do. Whatever the cause, we must find the strength to pray and go on. Take heart, dear one. Jesus wept for his friend Lazarus, and He weeps for you.

Name your pain. Is there a storm coming? Are you under a high or low pressure? Have you had surgery? Put a name to what you are feeling. "*Rainstorm Ethel* is breaking down my strength today, and I don't feel too good" is something I would tell my husband (hubs) when explaining why I'm not coping well on a certain day. This shows I have named the rainstorm as my problem. We joke with names. I have a short toe due to surgery, and it has been named Shorty. Hubs will ask me, "Is Shorty hurting today? Are we in for a weather change?"

Pray that God will lead you to some prayer warriors to help you at this time. Pray that you would develop an attitude of finding humor, even when the days (and nights) seem to stretch out before you. Pray constantly. Blessings and gentle hugs, even in times of struggles, dear friend.

DAY 9

"In" Sight

But his body pains him, And he mourns only for himself.

—Job 14:22 (NASB 1994)

WE REACH A time when all the smiles, all the displayed joy, and all the "I'm okays" fade, and we must be careful not to turn into ourselves. We do not always want to; however, the pain that we are in becomes almost too much to bear.

We have been suffering from our afflictions more then we care to remember. We long for just one day, nay, one hour of relief. We seek only someway to escape what is going on within our bodies and heads, and yet…the relief never comes. So we become self-absorbed. This is when we need to be careful. Your Goliath is breathing down your neck. Beware and be cautious, dear friend.

When the pain is too much to bear, we look to pills to help us escape. Our doctors may have told us that "you will not become addicted to this medication. It is needed for your condition." Well, I hate to say this, but we WILL become addicted. Pain medication to the chronic sufferer is just like alcohol to the alcoholic, just like the racetrack, Wall Street, or the lottery to the gambler, food to the bulimic or glutton. Anything can become an addiction. Once our body becomes adjusted to this medication, we will need more and more to take the edge of the pain away. Some days, we will think we should stop this medication. Other days, we are in a fog because we have had to take too much.

So how do we deal with all of this? We try to keep ourselves "IN sight" while the doctors are busy giving out pills of all kinds, not just pain pills, right and left. While family and friends question what is going on with us, they do not see the Goliath we have upon us. We may find that the pain is not as bad when we focus on something else. Try to find pleasure in other things. Take a walk if able. Paint a picture. Paint rocks. (David had rocks to throw at Goliath.) Read. Learn a new craft—knit, crochet, sew, or even try needle point or embroidery. Maybe take a stab at fly-fishing, a chess match or painting.

Pray that you will find strength to stay focused on what is around you and not your pain. Ask God to help you when you do become "IN" focused and show you how to find a way to see all that is good around you. Blessings and gentle hugs today, dear friend.

DAY 10

A Classic Whiner

Then the Lord said, "Is it right for you to be angry?"

—Jonah 4:4 (NKJV)

THERE IS A character in the Bible named Jonah. Even if you are not a regular church attender or Bible reader, you will probably know the story of Jonah and the whale. A man that was swallowed by a whale—really?

This may be one of the best examples in the Bible of a wimpy whiner that we have. This man was sitting on the front lines of God's battlefield. Yet he did nothing but run and hide because he did not approve of the battle that God had called him to! He went to such extremes as being willing to drown for his beliefs instead of fighting and living for God. Once in the water, and we know this, a big fish swallowed him for three days, then vomited him out, not just spit him out but vomited him out. And where did this happen? On the shores that God wanted Jonah to go to. Hello, Nineveh!

So Jonah preached to the peoples of Nineveh then exited the town. He went and sat on a hilltop and started whining all over again. Good grief!

We all know someone like this. Whine. Wine. Whine. Wine. You get to the point that you want to ask if they would like "a little cheese with their wine." They complain about things so much that it gets to be that their illness is no longer the only thing that is a problem. Life can never be good enough for these individuals. Everything that is going on with them is a drama.

When we were first diagnosed with our illness, yes, we talked a lot about it. But there is a time to let that go. Pick one or two family members or friends that you can count on to share your struggles with and stick to that. Do not whine to anyone else. Three days in the belly of a big fish for being a classic whiner would not be the ideal way to spend your time. And besides, you will stink when you come forth!

Pray. Ask God to hear your prayers from His home on high. Ask God to remove from you the sounds and stench of whining over your illness, to provide for you someone that can hear you on days that are hard and rejoice with you on days that are good. Blessings and gentle hugs to you, for you are a strong person and not a whiner.

DAY 11

Barbed-Wire Barrier and Hot-Tempered Man

Do not make friends with a hot tempered person,
do not associate with one easily angered.

—Proverbs 22:24 (NIV)

THERE ARE TIMES in my life that I have been an absentee church attender. Sometimes a month can go by. Once, however, there was a lapse of almost three years. This was a culmination of my health, my husband's heart issues, and subsequent surgery, but more to do with a church we had been attending and suddenly had to depart.

A hot-tempered man called me on not one but on three occasions and ripped out my heart regarding church business. Why did he have to do the yelling and screaming over the phone at me? Why the ranting and raving?

It was like he had put up a barbed wire fence between him and me, and we were not going to be able to serve together. He knew of my abilities from twenty years' service in another state. I had to wonder if that was the problem. Was there some jealousy going on? Back to the phone calls…

This pastor would not talk to my husband. He would only talk to me. I take that back; he didn't talk. He would shriek, thunder, scream, yell, storm, rant, and rave. I could tell that he was blue in the face even over the phone.

My husband came to my rescue and told this hot-tempered man that he would not talk to me like that, and we would no longer attend his church.

Sometimes you have to remove yourself from the line of fire. It might be family that is hot-tempered or friends, but you must remove yourself from the situation for your health.

Your treasure and peace are in God. Pray. Ask for this treasure today. Pray. Ask for the peace. Then hot-tempered people and barbed wire barriers will no longer be an issue for you. Blessings and gentle hugs for you today, dear friend.

DAY 12

Sick and Tired of Being Sick and Tired

I am exceedingly afflicted; Revive me,
O Lord, according to Your word.

—Psalm 119:107 (NASB 1995)

WE REACH A point in our illness that we feel we are just completely crushed down. We are sick and tired all the time. This is when we catch ourselves becoming sick of spirit and tired of belief that anything will ever change. We have days that we have some energy and enjoy our family and even some company. But those days are so few and far between that we fear making plans or promises. Then our spirit once again becomes tired, and you have an emotional breakdown and withdrawal.

You seek the comfort of a favorite pillow or blankie (or both), your beverage of choice. (Just a gentle reminder that artificial sweeteners are not friendly for most chronic illnesses, and neither are alcoholic beverages. Sorry.) For me, I sink into my spot on the sofa, cover up with my blankie, and in goes a video from my favorite TV series. As I have gotten many years under my belt with the disease (fibro), the bad days are fewer and farther apart, but they do still come. Why? We have no control over weather, which can really affect me, and other outside influences. In the early days however, the story was quite different. I hadn't learned my limits yet.

Several years ago, I attended a concert, featuring a Christian artist, Carman (Licciardello), when he returned to the stage after cancer treatment. My husband and I saw him in a small venue in Arkansas. I was also thankful to attend, as my daughters and I had gone to many of his concerts when he was very active in the 1980s and 1990s. We sang his songs at the top of our lungs. We loved Carman. And when he disappeared from the stage, we were devastated.

Back to this concert however…

Carman sang a song titled "Jesus Heal Me."[1] He asked for anyone that needed healing to stand, and he basically sang this song as a prayer over us. He sang this song and prayed **over me!** Carman is now with the Lord in paradise as he passed in 2021.

The words are so profound. (You can find it on YouTube.) Take in the words of this prayer. Jesus can heal, but you have to seek His face. You have to understand that *His healing* is in *His way and in His time*.

Jesus was the Master of miracles. And He is still in the miracle business! Jesus is the Great Physician. Many of the incidents of Jesus healing someone are recorded in the Bible. We know the references of Jesus and the paralyzed man. His friends brought him to Jesus and lowered him through the roof to reach Jesus. How about the lady that just reached out and touched His garment? She wanted healing and had faith that He would heal her through that simple touch. Oh, to be able to touch His garment today! Jesus raised the dead, touched the sick, brought sight to those that were blind, helped the lame to walk, and drove demons out of those afflicted with craziness.

If Jesus did all that, couldn't He heal any of us with a chronic disease? Find a renewed strength in your faith today. I know today may be a hard day for you. I know the pain is crushing you down sometimes. But Jesus is there, ready to hold you. He has His Nail-Scarred Hands, open to help with the pain. Seek His face. He will hold you. He will comfort you. There is no guarantee that you will be cured. Prayers are answered four ways: yes, no, maybe, and later or not yet. Can you deal with those kinds of answers? Whatever His answer is for your prayer of healing, hold onto His garment. Rest in

---

[1] "Jesus Heal Me" by Carman, on album *No Plan B*, released by Norway Avenue Records, Carman World Outreach, Inc., 2014. This information is provided by Carman Licciardello's official website.

those Nail-Scarred Hands on those bad, hard days. Pray today and remember to thank Him on the days that you feel even a little bit better. Keep a journal of your prayers and how they are answered. When you see that God is giving you more and more good days, does your heart and spirit begin to overflow and rejoice? Blessings and gentle hugs, dear friend.

DAY 13

A Cocoon

Woe is me for my hurt! My wound is severe. But I say,
"Truly this is an infirmity, and I must bear it."

—Jeremiah 10:19 NKJV

I DON'T KNOW about you and your walk with your disease or illness, but there are days that I feel about as good as that nasty see-through toilet paper you find in so many public bathrooms, like you could see, deep inside me, if I were held up to a light. There is only one light I want to be held up to, and that is the light of Jesus Christ. Yet there are those days—I call them my cocoon days.

And cocoon days remind me of butterflies, which I truly love. I have often tried to have a butterfly garden, but to no avail. The flowers die, and the butterflies are few and far between. I love watching them. They give me a sense of peace, watching them flutter around with their fragile wings, their beauty, and their grace. For those of us walking with a disease or illness that knows no end, we too will have our cocoon days, followed by days when we open up our fragile wings and attempt to fly. Cocoon days are when the bottom has fallen out of our life's well, days when all we can do is curl up into our self and recharge. Maybe it is a few days, maybe a week. Whatever it is, this is a time for Restoration. Rejuvenating. Reinstatement. Revival. Reconstruction.

Jesus had several "cocoon" moments in His life, times He would withdraw from the disciples and crowds to be wrapped in the arms of His Father. He began His life on earth being swaddled in His mother's arms, cocooned in her holy wrap. His ministry began only a few short years later when Jesus taught the leaders at age twelve. He was left behind on Passover. Was this a mistake or a mission? Mission. His actual ministry began years later after going into the mountains for a time of prayer and fasting, cocooned by His Father and the holy angels from all around Him. There were times He would have to recharge from the aches of His days and His ministry while He prepared for another sermon, series of ministry, or miracles. The last cocoon moment for our Lord came as He was being removed from the cross, cleaned up, and placed in a borrowed tomb. The burial sheet was wrapped tight around Him. And the stone was rolled over the opening.

But this is not the end of the story (as we used to hear on the radio). Miracle of miracles, Jesus is no longer in the tomb! Even when we emerge from our cocoons, we carry scars just as Jesus carries the scars of the cross. We carry the scars of pain, both physical and emotional. We often drag out our scars frequently with a poor, poor, pitiful me attitude, waiting on someone to take care of us, waiting on someone to be our hero. Jesus is there to be that hero. Remember, Jesus is alive!

Pray. Ask God to heal you. Understand that healing may not be full body, or it may mean your spirit. You will have scars to bear, but know that Christ, and Christ alone, understands the scars you carry. Ask God to use your scars and illness as a testimony to His great joy and glory. Know that your scars may be meant to stay hidden. Blessings and gentle hugs, dear friend, as you emerge from your cocoon as something beautiful. And have a wonderful day!

DAY 14

Feasting on the Good

Every day is hard for those who suffer, but a
happy heart is like a continual feast.

—Proverbs 15:15 (NCV)

WE ARE OVERWHELMED with food everywhere we look. It is on television, in magazines, even in pop-ups on social media. We must shop for food, prepare, and then clean up after said food is eaten. We have to throw out spoiled food and look the other way should someone be sick from our food. But we should also feast on other things, such as God's Word.

Feasting during the holidays causes pain to our digestion and agony to our psyche afterward. But there is one feasting that we can relish in with no discomfort later. In fact, this feast will leave us reaching for the mark.

Feast on the words of God and His holy book, the Bible. Prepare for yourself a list of verses that you can go to when you are having your bad days, your "cocoon days," your "tempted to be a whiner" days. You know those days. They sneak up on you and smack you like WHAM!

In my own feasting of the word, I found that Exodus was one of my favorite books. I love Exodus, how God took the Israelites through the journey to the promised land, an eleven-day journey turning into forty years. Yet God provided all along the way. But what did the Israelites do? Cry and whine. Moan and groan. Have we learned anything from them? Not much at all! What is your favorite book in the Bible?

I love the book of Ruth. Four chapters. "I will go where you go." It is a marvelous read. What is your favorite passage in the Bible?

One of my favorite verses is John 11:35, "Jesus wept." What are five of your favorite verses?

Have you looked at any of these lately? Spent any time with them lately? Remember, you can come to the table and feast at any time. We are not limited in our access to our Father. Pray. Ask God to feed you a bountiful feast each time you come to His table. Ask Him to fill you over and over again. Blessings and gentle hugs as you come to the table, dear friend.

DAY 15

To Endure All

The will to live can get you through sickness,
but no one can live with a broken spirit.

—Proverbs 18:14 (NCV)

I HAVE TO wonder what is up with my legs. My restless leg syndrome is so bad that sometimes I wish there was a little section of my brain that could be zapped to turn off this disease. I have to wonder what is up with my head and hands. I have essential tremor disorder, also known as ET. I shake to the point that I cannot even eat with a spoon on most days. Talk about being embarrassed. Remember the mess your toddler made with her/his spoon learning how to eat? I'm almost that good. Eating with large family gathering is such fun. (NOT!)

My luck though is that the area of the brain that needs to be adjusted would be right next to the "overeating" area, or it would be next to the "be a slob" area. Maybe it would be next to a "don't shower today, dude," area. And the laser would hit one of these instead of the spot that needed to be rectified.

I have tried to learn how to deal with these issues, as I cannot take a lot of supplements or medications. Imagine that—allergies to everything! I increase my potassium naturally, take hot showers, and use a heating pad on top of my blankets. There are nights that I sleep in my recliner with the heating pad over my legs. I do this so I can carry on the next day.

When you lose sleep for whatever reason, you are starting the next day below the best you can be. What is it that affects you? A migraine that has lasted for several hours or days, just finished chemo or radiation sessions that leaves you feeling weak, ill, and totally wiped out, or maybe you are just having one of those days with your illness. Our verse today says we can live through sickness. But we have to have a strong will to live, to survive, to know that we are survivors. You are a survivor. But if your spirit becomes broken…

Have you ever felt the weight of the world crushing you down? That is living with a broken spirit. Believe me when I say, "We are doing the best we can," so stop being so hard on yourself. Stop putting yourself down and looking to the past with an "if only" attitude. There is a fine line however between focusing on self for health reasons and focusing on self to be self-serving and whiny. We need to stop and look in the mirror and think about the past and all the things we used to do, then realize all the good we are able to do where we are now. Look in the mirror again and say, "I am going to make it! I am strong and wonderfully made!"

Pray. Seek a new outlook and a renewal for your smile, all the way to your eyes. Blessings and gentle hugs, my dear friend. Smile!

DAY 16

How Serious?

And his sickness was so serious that there was no breath left in him.

—1 Kings 17:17b (NKJV)

WHEN WAS THE last time you had your breath taken away from you? Hopefully, it was in a good way. Were you surprised by an aha moment of love, life, and excitement? Nonetheless all too often, with a chronic illness, our breath is taken away with the pain and sometimes just by getting through everyday life. I recently had to experience the painful need of having injections in both of my knees to try and delay knee replacement surgery yet once again. Oh, how these injections take my breath away, and not in a good way. But through all this, I (we) need to try to embrace life. Embrace life? Through that kind of pain, you ask? Have your breath taken away from hurts and pains? Oh, dear friend, yes. Because if you get lost in the pain, you will never find the ah-ha moments and have life abundant.

So what is life abundant? We all have it, even if you do not believe that. Life abundant is everyday life—the taxes, rat race, birthdays, anniversaries, being stuck in traffic, coffee spilling, rising grocery costs, and candlelight dinners. Life abundant—it is everyday life. It is what we live and how we seek to live. Plant some flowers. Remember your good fortune of a car trip without getting in an accident. Do you know how rare that is? Are you able to purchase your medicine? Did you find a parking spot close to the door at the mall, grocery, pharmacy, or doctor's office? Do you know how rare that is? This is life abundant.

God grants us favor each and every day. We need to open our eyes to all that He brings to us. Keep a diary, or write on a slip of paper, and start a "blessings jar." Put those slips of paper in the jar when you have a blessing or joy. Then on the days that are bad, you can read them and know that you do have good days. You will see that God is working in your life.

When you first get bad news, such as your health, you want to lament and cry, then wallow like a pig in mud. Your family and friends will only want to hear this for so long. Then you may go into a time of mourning—mourning the life you lost. Be happy—happy that God will carry you through and bring you to ah-ha moments. If in pain, put on your big girl or big boy pants and deal with it. If you have to go to a separate room, take a pain pill of some kind and just chill for a few moments. Do it. Then get back to life. You will find that exercise is a big help, as are showers.

Pray. Ask God to provide you with more joyous moments. They will help keep you free from depression over your illness, which Goliath just wants to pour down on you. There are some medications that cover both depression and chronic pain. So if this is an issue for you, you might want to ask your doctor. I AM NOT suggesting that you take medications. But many of us with a chronic illness also suffer from SAD (seasonal affective disorder). Blessings, gentle hugs, and life abundant today, dear friend.

Endurance

Woe to me because of my brokenness—I am severely wounded!
I exclaimed, "This is my intense suffering and I must bear it."

—Jeremiah 10:19 (HCSB)

By now, if your illness is fairly new, you are still learning about your body, the illness, and ways to deal with it. You are discovering your "wall" (known as the slamming down on the endurance level in a split second), of your pain levels. You are also learning how your body will react to weather.

Oh, we do not love weather at all! I don't care if you are newbie "fibromite," have nerve pain, and migraines. Do you suffer from Crohn's or celiac disease? Lactose intolerance can wreak havoc on many of us! Maybe you are a new adventurer in the field of arthritis, be it rheumatoid or osteoarthritis (most common). Gout? Whatever your chronic illness is, even the more experienced of us will suffer from SAD (seasonal affective disorder). High-pressure systems really bother me. But for you, it may be the low-pressure system. Or bless your heart, it may be both. Get a weather report system that shows the barometric pressure so you can begin to track it. Once you get a hold on how you react, you will know what to expect.

Maybe you are a "graduate" to the regular section in the doctor's office. Good thing? Bad thing? Who knows. No one other than you have learned how your body responds to many things. You know your "wall." You know how you react to weather. But there are many other things that may have developed by now: food allergies, medicine allergies, latex allergy. It is like you are running a race with your health, and the road is filled with potholes. (And we all know how well potholes are filled in, don't we?) You have sleeping issues and bowel issues. Do I need to continue?

Hello to the caretaker. I do not want to leave you out. You have your days of feeling broken and exhausted. You have your days of being angry that your mate/family member has this disease (diseases). Your life together has been changed, and you feel cheated. You have days of playing nursemaid because your mate cannot get out of the bed, except for personal reasons. So you prepare meals, clean the kitchen, encourage, love, wipe tears, and hold. And who encourages and loves on you? God is there for you too, my dear friend. Do not turn your back. Do not let this Goliath steal the joy from your household.

We miss out on family events, favorite pastimes, lunch dates with the gang. Once you have a good hint of your body, the strength and endurance you have, you need to be the one scheduling any of the activity that you are involved in. This way, you can use wisdom for running your race and be more involved with your family and friends. Bring back your joy. Bring back the abundance in your life. Remember to schedule times of rest, or you will crash and hit your wall.

Pray. Ask for strength to run the race, even when there are potholes. You can do it. I know you can. And so does God! Blessings and gentle hugs, dear friend.

DAY 18

Abide with Trust

Then Jesus turned to the Jews who had claimed to believe
in him. "If you stick with this, living out what I tell you,
you are my disciples for sure. Then you will experience
for yourselves the truth, and the truth will free you."

—John 8:31–32 (MSG)

According to *Webster's Dictionary*, abide means "to endure without yielding; withstand; tolerate; to await." I like the definition that *Webster's* uses for "to await"—to await on the coming of the Lord. Can you abide in the trust of Christ until the coming of the Lord? There are many things we have to take care of before those days are here. Even now, there are many that say the end of days are upon us. I'll get to more of that a little later. But for now, back to our illness and trust…

Your illness is like Goliath. How do you overcome Goliath? With a slingshot and a stone. How do we overcome? Letting God hold us and show us how we can be overcomers. We abide in Him, proclaiming that He is our stronghold. We become able to withstand. We are able to endure without yielding—you know, those yield signs that no one pays any attention to anyway.

We won't stay down in the pits where our pain can pull us. We won't let the depression drag us to the gates of oblivion. We won't let the pain put us in potholes that refuse to be filled. We will not let the loneliness of the disease grab us and wrap ugly arms around us.

Now, back to the end of days, as I mentioned earlier. Some say, we have already had many of the signs and wonders of the end of days. But folks, we do not know when the Lord will return. We just need to be ready!

> Now concerning how and when all this will happen, dear brothers and sisters, we don't really need to write you, For you know quite well that the day of the Lord's return will come unexpectedly, like a thief in the night.

—1 Thessalonians 5:1–2 (NLT)

We need to stay in His Word. We need to be hungry for what the Word will fill us up with. Read Daniel and Revelation, and find a good Bible-based church. You will find that your love hunger is filled.

We will open our eyes, take our first steps, just like a toddler branching out. We will become the overcomer God wants us to be and know that our illness will not get us down. Goliath will not be the winner at this time. We will be happy, strong, and joyful. Why? Because we will experience the truth, and the truth will set us free! Pray. Ask for strength and happiness. Ask for the knowledge to become an overcomer and the Goliath slayer. Blessings and gentle hugs to you, my dear friend.

DAY 19

The Potter and the Clay

But now O Lord, You are our Father; We are the clay, and
You our potter; And all of us are the work of your hand.

—Isaiah 64:8 (NKJV)

HAVE YOU EVER played in clay? I, for one, do not enjoy working in clay
and pottery. I do not like cutting things off a pottery wheel. I do not
like the dryness my hands feel after all the working, kneading, shaping,
and twisting, all the molding and pulling. And then there is the even-
tual firing. Glaze and coat, enter into the kiln, pray and hope that what
you have created comes out in the iconic beauty you have designed. I
have a granddaughter that is quite skilled at pottery. She has her own
wheel and has made numerous vessels as gifts for family members. Her
actions have made me wonder about our Lord working on us. He is,
after all, our potter, as our verse today states. On the wheel we go again
and again as He sees the changes and corrections we need in our lives.

As children, we did the same thing by playing in the mud, making mud pies, mud forts, mud roads for trucks and armies, dams and
rivers. We maneuvered the mud where we wanted it to go.

As an adult, my house is no less fascinating regarding mud. There
is a bird called cliff swallows that has decided to build its nests under
the eaves of my house just at the front door. These obnoxious little birds
build a nest one dab of mud at a time, under the eaves of a bridge, a
home, buildings. And they do not build just one nest. They build col-
onies. Imagine ten or twelve nests built one mud dab at a time on your
home! Dare I say that I am not open to this colony at my front door.

The verse above is no less directing. The Lord is the Potter. He is the One that is in control of the shape we are in. He is the one that molds us, twists us, turns us, and kneads us. We are the clay. We are at His beck and call. We are the ones that are lying in His Nail-Scarred Hands and letting Him have His way with us. Do you lie still and let the Lord have His way with you when you are in His Nail-Scarred Hands? Why or why not? (Answer.)

How many times have you felt that you have been put through the fire? _______________________

I know I have been through the fire more than once! Sometimes I feel like I must not be learning the lesson, that I have new things to learn, or I have bumps to be smoothed out. And the ever-present work that the Father deems appropriate for us to have done and go through the fire for. You see, we are all—yes, ALL work of His hand. And when He deems that it is time to work on us, we better take notice.

So I ask you, where are you in your walk with the Father? What are you doing in your service? How are you doing with your quiet time? Are you tithing? Now, I realize some of these may be difficult for everyone all the time. But you are responsible to the Lord for your answers. You see, there was a time I could not tithe my 10 percent, but I started at just $5 per paycheck and moved up to a percentage quickly. Some days, I am not able to serve. I do good to take care of my personal needs. So there you have it. Pray. Ask for guidance when you are not in the fire and understanding when it is time to go through the fire once again. Help me choose to serve the Potter. Blessings and gentle hugs today, dear friend.

Fighting Your Goliath

Then David put his hand in his bag and took out a stone:
and he slung it, and struck the Philistine on his forehead,
so that the stone sank into his forehead, and he fell on his
face to the earth. So David prevailed over the Philistine
with a sling and a stone, and struck the Philistine and killed
him. But there was no sword in the hand of David.

—1 Samuel 17:49–50 (NKJV)

GOLIATH STACKED UP to nine feet nine inches in today's measure-
ments. David was a huge five feet. Goliath was wrapped in armor.
David was dressed in lion skins, as was normal for a shepherd.
Goliath's voice was that of two angry boom boxes at full volume,
fighting each other in the same area. Imagine a very, very angry green
giant, protecting his veggies against one lone Keebler elf.

This is the battle we face. We are David, facing this giant in our
walk with our illness. We have good days when the giant is quiet. But
then we have days when the GIANT raises his ugly head, and we feel
the battle all over again. So how do we conquer the giant on those
days? OH my!

The battle between David and Goliath took place between two
mountains, down in the valley—deep down in the valley. Sound
familiar? How often are we down in a valley? You know those valleys:
the pain, shakes, tremors, bumblebees stinging throughout our body,
depression, muscle cramps, fatigue. The list goes on and on and on.
You know, if we never have a **test** like David did, we would not have

a **test**imony. For forty days, Goliath had yelled at the army of the Israelites every morning and every evening. Sound familiar with your disease, hitting you at all hours? Are you ready to take a stone and a slingshot to your Goliath?

So how will you conquer your Goliath? Pick up your sling (the Bible), find your stone for the day (your verse), and throw the stone with all you've got at your Goliath. Let him know that you are standing with God. Let Goliath know that today you are up, and you are ready to take this day by a slingshot and a stone!

Yes, it takes work. A Goliath is like that. It is strong, but only as strong as you allow it to be. It is powerful, but only as powerful as you allow it to be. It is hurtful, but only as hurtful as you allow it to be. Pray. Ask for the strength of Goliath but the gentleness of David, remembering he did not use a sword but a slingshot and a stone. David had faith in his God. Do you? Blessings and gentle hugs today, dear friend. Gentle hugs.

SECTION 2

Remembering that God is on Your Side

Restoration

He gives power to the weak, and to those who
have no might He increases strength.

—Isaiah 40:29 (NKJV)

How often do we have the chance to be refreshed and restored? Some of us can go on vacation with the hopes and the thoughts of being refreshed and restored. So often, however, when we get home, we need several days to recharge our batteries before getting back into our routines, and then, sometimes, just getting back into our routines is just what restores the balance for us.

How blessed are those of us that have been restored by the loving grace of our Lord Jesus Christ. He is, after all, the Great Physician. When we need that healing grace, who else do we call on but the Great Physician for this kind of restoration? When I am sitting at the feet of the King, I know that I am truly restored. I do not have to fear the arrows being thrown around about me. I do not have to fear the pains that are coming from within or without. I know that I can leave my bed and stand with my King and be wholly well.

It is like using a refresh body cloth on your illness…a magic eraser, and it is gone. Can you do this? If you have the faith of a mustard seed, you can. But sometimes, faith waivers. Continue in prayer, and keep the refresh cloths handy. Invest in your health. For you see, there are days, as you well know, that we wake up, and our strength is weak. There are days, and we wake up, and our strength is strong. Whatever the day, shower, put on a comfortable outfit, your big girl panties or big boy pants on, and I add a touch of lipstick. Red. What can you do to refresh your day? You see, sometimes, everyone you meet says, "Gee, do you feel okay?" "Are you all right?" If you have a general tendency to see the glass as half empty, you will always see the glass as half empty. And hearing words like this, you will begin to think, *Oh, I must be sick.* Do you generally see the glass as half full? Good for you! You are the one that will see clouds in the sky and find the castles, elephants, hot dogs, horses, and hands. Don't look at the blowing and stirring clouds and assume that a storm is coming. Look for the silver lining. Look for your pot of gold in those clouds.

Restoration.   Rejuvenating.   Reinstatement.   Revival. Reconstruction—all of these are life-giving words. Do you find yourself in any of these words? They are God-given glory gifts to you. You are worthy of them. Do not feel that you are not. Remember, the darkest part of the night is always just before the dawn, and joy comes in the morning with the sunrise. So if the pain has built up, and the tears want to fall, fill a tub with warm water. Light candles. Turn on your fave tunes. And ease on down…ease on down…ease on down…ease on down.

Ahh.

Pray today. Ask God to keep you, to guide you, to restore you, to revive you, to help you stand strong on days you are weak, and to show you how to grow stronger every day. Blessings and gentle hugs every day, dear friend.

DAY 22

Strength

I can do all things through Christ who strengthens me.

—Philippians 4:13 (NKJV)

"I AM WOMAN. Hear me roar."[2] My three girlfriends and I performed a comedy act to this in a high school talent show. It was such a success that we ended up performing at the other high schools in our city. If you are old enough, you are humming the lyrics in your head. If you have never heard of this song, don't worry about it! Haha.

I am a woman, or you may be a man. It does not matter. A chronic illness is equal opportunity. Race doesn't matter. Neither does creed. Creed? What the heck is creed? We always hear people say that—race, color, or creed.

Creed, according to the dictionary, is (1) "the formal statement of Christian beliefs, especially the Apostles Creed," (2) "then they will swear that they believe in the creed and the commandments."

I can do ALL things through Christ. I am a woman. Some may ask, where does it end? Well, be thankful it doesn't. Be thankful that Christ is there for all things. He strengthens us for each day, every hour, all moments of our life. Christ is the strength giver and the wish maker. We don't have to stand on stage and roar. (Although some of us enjoy the limelight.)

---

2 "I Am Woman," written by Helen Reddy and Ray Burton, recorded in 1971, released in May 1972 (Capitol Records) (Google Internet services).

There are famous people with fibro, and yet they do not speak out. There is a National Fibromyalgia Network, yet the numbers are few. There are limited medications. There are many other chronic illnesses that have famous people that could speak out with the disease, yet they do not. The numbers are too few. One is pseudotumor cerebri—one in one hundred thousand. How do we get people to take a stand for all of these illnesses when there are so many? Let our numbers be counted! Come out in strength as a group and as a single person. Remember that through Christ, I can do all things. Pray today that you will find your roar dear friend. Ask for the strength that allows you to do all things. Blessings and gentle hugs.

The Good News

Yet the news about Him spread all the more, so that crowds of people came to hear Him and to be healed of their sicknesses.

—Luke 5:15 (NIV)

As many of us may have read and studied the four gospels in our churches and on our own, we have learned how the news of Jesus had spread throughout the lands that surrounded the Sea of Galilee, Palestine, Bethlehem, and Jerusalem. Jesus had performed so many signs and miracles that the news brought people from far and wide. Jesus healed the sick, changed water into wine, made the blind to see, and healed the crippled. He removed demons, fed five thousand plus with two loaves of bread and five fish. His touch cured the woman tarnished with the flow of blood. And His second-to-last miracle was to raise His friend Lazarus from the dead. Oh, how we need this kind of good news today!

We have rallies filled with anger, loud voices, and frustration. We have riots filled with hate, brutality, and violence. We have people that are hurting, broken, and needing someone to pay attention to them. We have indignation and rage coming from the right, the left, the middle. It is coming from every angle in between. Oh, how do we reach them? We don't! But there is one that can!

I remember back when my youngest daughter was in the first grade and talking to me while I was preparing dinner. She was jabbering on and on, and I was answering in what I thought was all the correct spots with an "uh-huh" or an "oh, wow." Finally, this little gal had had enough, and she reached over to me (she was sitting on the kitchen counter), and she put her little hands on my cheeks and said to me, "Momma, listen to me!" Feeling like dirt, I told her I was listening. She said, with hands still on my face, "Momma, listen to me with your eyes!" How often do we do that, listen with our ENTIRE attention—our face, our posture, our time, our everything?

You see, God does. He listens with everything. But in today's world of the cell phone, iPad, Facebook, and TikTok, just to name a few, who needs to listen IN PERSON anymore? People under the age of thirty-five struggle to know what it is like to go without any of these items as a daily possession. Give these individuals a push button or dial phone, and many are not sure how to use it. What happened with face-to-face time? Talking about our joys and heartaches? Facing a problem head-on? Accepting criticism? They are not able to use words such as "I'm not myself today because," "I have been hurt by," "This feels very traumatic for me because." Everything is toxic, causes anxiety, and creates feelings that are oppressive. Face-to-face confrontation is something this group does not know how to handle. But how would this age group handle meeting Jesus in Jerusalem today?

When Jesus entered Jerusalem on Passover week, He was greeted with palm branches and alms. He was honored. Then He was given over in exchange for a murderer. How short the memories of His followers. Are our memories any better? We read passages of the Bible; we hear sermons over and over again; yet we seem to become numb to the words and the meanings. It's as if we were hearing or reading *The Three Little Pigs* or *Henny Penny*.

Where is our faith? Where is our joy of the good news? Do we share this good news? How excited are you when you get an actual phone call or a real piece of mail from a family member or friend? I know, for me, it thrills my heart. It lifts me up for several days.

Our Heavenly Father is no different. He is waiting to hear from you today. He wants to hear from us. He loves "knee mail," "praise mail," and "service mail." So, no, the sky is not falling, but mercy and grace may be. Pray. Ask God to fill your cup with His mercy and grace today. Ask God to help you seek His face throughout the day. Blessings and gentle hugs today, dear friend.

DAY 24

When the World Collapsed

But know this, that in the last days perilous times will come.

—2 Timothy 3:1 (NIV)

THE YEAR 2020 brought to our globe a pandemic of science-fiction movie fare. It hit my local area the second week of March, one week after my husband had his heart surgery. So thankful that he had his surgery. Many did not get to have surgery after the pandemic started.

People went crazy loading up on toilet paper and cleaning supplies. My question was then and still is, number one, they couldn't eat the toilet paper and, number two, didn't they already clean? I couldn't understand the need to empty the store shelves so bad that others could not buy anything and trying to find antibacterial hand wash and scrub. It was a nightmare! My husband and I had to purchase for his parents and my mom to keep them home and safe. Most stores had a limit on things of one per family, so we would get two carts. We were, after all, shopping for multiple families. Our shopping trips would take up to eight hours sometimes just to get the items needed in all our homes for just a week. And if we found any kind of paper product or cleaning supply, we considered it a big win for that trip! I used to enjoy scavenger hunts, but wearing a mask and gloves and searching and scratching out our existence is not my idea of a warm party scavenger hunt.

The pandemic put an extra strain on any of us with a chronic illness. Some of us were often without some of our medications. This was a new situation for us after years of being able to get our medications at the drop of a hat. We also could no longer get to the senior center for our easy yoga classes to help with movement, stretching, and community. We could no longer get into the warm pool at the center for swimming, walking, and gentle weight lifting. Our world had collided, and we didn't have an outlet for those days or times. Instead, many ate. Many across the globe ate during the pandemic. We took online classes to make homemade pasta, bake bread, make soups and stews, bake pies, cakes, cookies, and other pastries. For us, extra weight means extra pain. And the cycles grow. We abuse ourselves. Why did I eat that? Why can't I lose that? We must realize that a lot of our medications cause us to not only gain weight but to harbor it like a long-lost friend. That is why, those exercise classes were so good for us. Do not beat yourself up over this as there is nothing you can do about it. It is medications, life, and the situation. Try making friends with your body for the time being.

Many people began to fear. Many began to hoard. Many began to think that the world was coming to an end. But ultimately, we have to remember that God is in control. When God created the world some thousands plus years ago, He knew that this pandemic would hit. I mean, after all, He was looking down through time. Do you really think this bug hit in 2020 and took God by surprise? HELLO! He knew what would cause it. He knew where it would begin. And He knew how it would all end.

Believe that God is here to provide protection. He knew at the beginning. And hands down, God went above and beyond to protect us. So where did your trust lie? In the mask you wore, the gloves you wore, the home you stayed in, or in the Lord, your God?

Pray today thanking God that there is no fear for the disease, the pandemic, the nightmare, God is in control. Blessings and gentle hugs, dear friend.

DAY 25

Bird Doo in Your Life?

Look at the birds of the air, for they neither sow nor
reap nor gather into barns; yet your heavenly Father
feeds them. Are you not of more value then they?

—Matthew 6:26 (NKJV)

WE EACH HAVE our own little quirks. Some of us may say "and" or
"so" all the time without even knowing it. Maybe we play with a
button, the hem of our garment, or change in our pocket if nervous.
Others of us may tend to wear the same color of socks on a given day,
not because that is their favorite color but because there is a need to
wear that color. (It may not even match the outfit.) Now, thanks to
the pandemic, many have to use every antibacterial pump they walk
by, not realizing the germs of people that have touched it.

For me, it's the birds, not the pretty birds that could be your
pets. It's the birds outdoors in nature that like to take a potshot at
me. Imagine this: walking out of McDonald's one spring morning
with your mother on your arm and a covered drink (thankfully) in
your hand. As you start across the parking lot, you hear this crazy
sound of a large plop. Looking down, there is bird excrement lying
on the lid of your beverage. Mother and I had tears of laughter running down our cheeks once we got over the surprise. Needless to say,
after I got Mom to the car, I went back into McDonald's, and they
were kind enough to replace the entire beverage, cup, and lid.

Episode two: I was on a mission trip with several teenage girls
and had taken them to the local pool for an afternoon break. As they

splashed and played, I relaxed on the side of the pool, soaking up some sun and reading. All of a sudden, this warm something spread across my back. Two of the girls saw and burst into giggles. The word spread like wildfire. Yep, bird doo.

Episode three: I was walking across a city square with some coworkers after lunch. I had an interview coming up that afternoon for a step-up position. You guessed it. On top of my balding head was a glorious bird doo. What a mess to clean up before that interview. Showing how I handled that help me land the job!

My car can be parked in an empty area of parking lots across the nation with no wires or trees around, and still it is like a beacon, calling out and asking to be hit. Recently, my house has become the newest casualty. Birds are trying to build nests on my front porch above my front door, then getting mad with my blowing it down and pooing on my porch. Hubs and I were out riding our Gold Wing (motorcycle). We were on a stretch of the highway that was empty of cars. Farmland spread as far as the eye could see on one side, rolling hills on the other side. Suddenly, I felt this warm ooze on my arm. I thought, *Really! All this space, and you have to hit me?* Then I just had to laugh, because why not? After all, I really am a magnet for a little bird doo every now and then.

Keep your chin up, your smile fresh, and above all, duck if you see birds coming! Pray and ask God to provide you with a sense of humor, a time of wonder, and the ability to laugh at yourself Blessings and gentle hugs today, dear friends.

He Was Wounded for Our Sins

But He was wounded for our transgressions, He was
bruised for our iniquities; the chastisement for our peace
was upon Him, and by His stripes we are healed.

—Isaiah 53:5 (NKJV)

DOES THIS VERSE just not make you tremble? Today is going to be
a little heavier than what we have been having, but hang with me,
okay? First, this verse is out of the book of Isaiah and is referring to
the crucifixion of Jesus. This is a foretelling of what would happen
to our Lord and Savior hundreds of years before it happened, years
before He was even born. How was that possible? Only through the
presence of God the Father speaking through Isaiah. Let's break this
verse apart and look at it in sections.

Part one: "He was wounded for our transgressions." He refers
to Jesus Christ, God, the Son, Emmanuel, the Holy One, I Am,
Jehovah, King of kings and Lord of lords, the Lamb of God, the
Light of the world, the Lion of Judah, Messiah, Prince of peace,
Rabbi, Redeemer, the resurrection and the life, our Shepherd.

He was wounded for us. Wounds. Hurts. Cuts. We all have
had wounds but nothing as deep as the wounds Jesus would have.
He would have wounds so deep; the sinew of His back and His sides
would show. He would have a cat o' nine tails dragged and whipped
across His back again and again and again until He had no breath left
in His body. Wounds…just for you; just for me.

Transgressions. Sin…plain and simple. Each morning. Every day. From the time we set our feet on the floor as we are getting out of bed, it starts. When Satan says, "Oh goody, she's/he's up," and he starts working. Those little white lies? Sin. Nine percent to church this time instead of tithing? Sin. Chatting about the "needs of Bobby Sue and Johnny" in the name of a prayer request that turns into gossip? Sin. It happens every day to all of us when we do not watch out.

Part two: "He was bruised for our iniquities." Jesus was bruised for us…for you and for me. If you are anything like me, you can wake up with a bruise and have no idea how it got there. Sometimes, I think I can get a bruise just walking through a room. I know that most of it is due to my medication. But Jesus? He was beaten with rods. He was beaten with staffs. He was beaten with tree branches. But He was not broken, because the Father would not allow a bone to be broken on our Lord. But bruised? Oh, the deep, dark bruise colors that took effect around His body, His face, His arms, His legs. Nothing was left untouched, all along the rips and tears of His body. It just makes my heart break when I think about my Jesus being treated this way.

Iniquities. What does this word even mean? It is the act of being mean, evil, unfair, wicked. Remember the mean girls from high school, those boys known as bullies? We sure see all this going on in our poor, tired world right now more than ever. But it is nothing more than sin—plain and simple. Have you been mean to someone today just because they were mean to you or because you thought they were mean to you? There is a lot of that going on in our world today, too much of it. Do you think "an eye for an eye" is the right way to live? What happened to compassion? Kindness? Gentleness? When did we stop treating people this way?

Part three: The chastisement for our peace was upon Him. Chastisement is another way of saying severely punished, whipped, beat. Without Jesus bearing the pain He did, we would not have the peace we do and the peace we will.

Part four: By His stripes, we are healed. For those of us suffering with a chronic illness, this part of the verse has special meaning. For all the population that believe, the stripes of Jesus are the healing of our sin. When we believe in the blood of Jesus and the resurrection of Jesus Christ, the stripes of our Lord bring us the healing of our saving grace. But as someone with a chronic illness, let's look at it this way also: the healing stripes of Jesus. Among the names of Jesus are Healer and Physician. His stripes are a healing balm to us. No, we may not have the full physical healing we want here on earth, but we can rest in the Nail-Scarred Hands and know that our Redeemer lives. He knows the pain and valleys we walk through each and every day of our lives, and He wants to take away our pain. He wants to walk with us and talk with us and touch us. He wants to teach us and spend time with us. When He was on the cross, He knew that His Nail-Scarred Hands would hold my fibro-worn body, and He would caress my restless leg–weary body, and He would say to me, "Tami, rest, my child. Rest." He can do that for you too, whatever your illness.

Pray. Ask God to help you walk with Him today. If you are not a child of God, ask Him to show you the stripes of your healing so you may see the great and wondrous signs that God has for you. He may not heal you, but He might. He will give you rest, such sweet rest. He will give you peace. Oh, so blessed will be your peace. And He will give you salvation, the wonderous grace of salvation. (There are verses at the front of this devotional that can help guide you to the gift of salvation.)

Pray this simple prayer with me today: Father, I ask You to come into my heart. I ask You to take away all my sins. I know that I am a sinner. I want to be Your child, Lord. I want to follow You. I want Your healing touch today. I know that doesn't mean a cure from my chronic illness, but it does mean I am healed from my sinful world and cleansed with Your blood. Amen.

If you prayed this simple prayer, we are so thankful! You are now a child of God. You are encouraged to find a local Bible-based church and get as involved as you are able. Write down the date here that you prayed this prayer, as Satan will try to tell you that you never prayed and got saved: ____

Blessings and gentle hugs for each and every one of you today, dear friend.

Be of Good Courage

Have I not Commanded you? Be strong and of good
courage; do not be afraid, nor be dismayed, for the
Lord your God is with you wherever you go.

—Joshua 1:9 (NKJV)

HAVE YOU EVER been dismayed? *Webster's Dictionary* describes dismay as "a feeling of being disappointed, discouraged, or upset." Who among us has not felt at least one of these? Dismayed. Oh, to know and remember God is on our side and to take hold of this feeling. To realize we can stand strong wherever we go. We feel dismayed most often in the midst of a storm, a storm that drains our strength, the strength of our emotions, our physical abilities, and our mental competence and effectiveness.

Our kids get dismayed all the time. "I don't want to clean my room," "I'm bored," "I don't want to eat THAT!" "You expect me to wear that!" And of course, the original, "Are we there yet?" As adults, we have our own issues and disappointments that we can count on almost daily. "Why don't we ever do anything," "You never take me anywhere," "That's not where I want to go for a vacation." We seem to grump more often than getting along. Why is that? We are dismayed. We are discouraged.

The Israelites took an eleven-day journey that turned into forty years of wandering…wandering, whining, groaning, demanding, and grumping through the desert, over the mountains, and through the valleys, hearing, "I'm tired of walking," "I want to go back to

Pharaoh," "I'm tired of eating manna all the time," "Why are we following this cloud and fire instead of going our own way?" Can you imagine dealing with over five thousand children and adults that whined all the time like this? Moses and Joshua had to have the strength of ten men, but God fed them what they needed. God was giving Joshua strength for the battle ahead. He could be giving us strength for the battles we are in. Moses did not cross into the promised land. After leading the Israelites for forty years, Moses's job was done. It was time for Joshua to take over.

Moses and Joshua knew that God was the Great I AM. Do you know this today? Yes, your illness may drag on for forty years. I have had mine for over twenty. I have prayed for healing. Your prayers are answered "yes," "no," "maybe," and "not now." Maybe there is good that can come from the load you now carry. Yes, the load may be heavy, and, dear friend, I do understand that. Yes, the load may seem unbearable at time(s), and I know that feeling. But God, the Great Physician, can take on our load. The Lord can give us courage.

This section is remembering that God is on your side. We have looked at strength and now courage. Pray, acknowledging God is the One that holds us in His Nail-Scarred Hands. Ask that He will be the one that gives you strength, courage, and fulfillment no matter what stage of your disease you are in. Blessings and gentle hugs today, dear friend.

Hand-Holding

For I, the Lord your God, will hold your right hand,
saying to you, "Fear not, I will help you."

—Isaiah 41:13 (NKJV)

THERE IS JUST something about physical touch that encourages us. No matter what some people say about not needing it, we all do. We all crave it. We all grow from it. Skin is the largest sensory organ we have. And, yes, for many of us, skin can be very tender. But still, we hunger for a love touch. It has been said by many, including studies from the Northwestern University medical school in Chicago and the University of Massachusetts, that a minimum of four hugs a day are required for physiological benefits. These benefits include a reduction of blood pressure to an increase in oxygen. Any of us with pain sensitivity can tell you that this will help to some degree with our pain level. The key to these hugs, however, are short, nonsuggestive hugs that last a minimum of seconds, conveying the message "I love you" to "I like spending time with you." Hugs really do speak louder than words.

Another way of getting in your "love touch" is hand-holding. This is considered such an old-fashioned form of showing one's love for each other. How often do we see older couples walking along the sidewalk, the beach, or elsewhere, out for an evening walk, holding hands? For those of us that are unsteady, the hand of a partner gives a feeling of strength and security. Date night with the one you love? Holding hands is like a secret pact that says, "You are mine, and I am yours." Having to hear bad news or go into a place that is unfamiliar, the hand of your loved one brings peace. Sitting down to dinner, at home, or out in public and taking hold of your partner's hand across the table to pray brings unity and hope...the love touch of hands.

We hold babies with them. We tuck our children in with them. We pat faces and kiss our children good night. We cannot wait to hold our grandchildren when we hear about them. We weave magic through the lives of our families every day with our hands and our love touch.

But there is not a touch any sweeter than the touch of the Nail-Scarred Hands. Oh, the love Jesus has for us...for you and for me. Oh, the touch of His hands. Just a reminder, He is the Great Physician. Why not let Him touch you today with His Nail-Scarred Hands, the touch of our hands entwined with His? Pray today. Ask for the love touch of the Nail-Scarred Hands. Ask that your spirit will be entwined with His in the hands of our Lord. Blessings and gentle hugs today, dear friend.

His Way Is Perfect

God is my strength and power, and He makes my way perfect.

—2 Samuel 22:33 (NKJV)

How often do we work in our own strength, only to find that we have been wasting extra time, energy and unwanted anguish when a simple turn in our step would have taken us to God? Oh, dear friend, if you are like me—too many times. We think we are on the correct path. The map is laid out before us. All the turns are marked, and we know each step of the way. But then, somehow, someplace, it all goes horribly wrong. And we spend countless hours, tears, and much heartache trying to undo that one misstep we took.

His way is perfect, lest we forget that. Perfect. One hundred percent. A+. Top of the class.

Could it have been His plan that we go this way? To stumble and fall? To experience this heartache and pain?

How many times did Peter stumble and fall, then became one of the greatest church leaders of the New Testament? How often did Jonah cry and hide, whine, and carry on before he carried the news to Nineveh? How bad did David mess up after killing Goliath? He fell from the perfect way of God. He even hid in a cave! Eventually, David became the king of Israel. But even then, his eyes wandered, his heart lusted, and his words caused death. Finally, he listened and became a man after God's own heart. What can one say about Job, a man that lost everything but stayed true to God even when his wife told him to curse God? When Job finally did question God, they had a heavy conversation, and God set Job straight.

Could God love any of us less than these? Could He use any of us less or more than these? Could He be teaching us a lesson any less than one of these? The answer is no, dear friend. God loves you. When we stumble and fall, don't hide in a dark closet. Pick yourself up, dust yourself off, and start again. The lesson is learned, and off you go. God's way is perfect. Maybe this path you are on was His path after all, and you HAD to learn this lesson for some reason. You may not know that reason just now, and you don't have to, for God's ways are perfect. One of these days, His reasons will come through to you, and all will become clear.

I can tell you, after graduating from the "school of hard knocks," I am a better witness for it. I can reach women who have been abused, for I have been in an abusive marriage. I can reach out to women that have had to bury a child, for I have had to bury a child due to cancer. I have had a prodigal child, resting in the swill of life before coming back to me and to God. I can guide and help women clawing their way through the valley of the prodigal grandchildren, as I have experienced grandchildren running away from home. While they have returned to the outskirts of the family, that doesn't include the grandparent. It's heartbreaking. Nothing worthwhile is ever easy. God remained my strength through it all, and He continues today. I have to say, I am thankful that He chose me to be His vessel and witness.

Pray today. Ask God to be there when you stumble and fall and start again. We all do it. But remember that God has a perfect plan for you. He, and He alone, is your strength and power, not pills, not crystals, not magic. God. He has a plan for you. It might not be today. It might not be tomorrow, but He will show you when the time is right, and your heart is aligned. Blessings and gentle hugs, dear friend.

DAY 30

Make Strong the Brick

Draw your water for the siege! Fortify your strongholds! Go into the clay and tread the mortar! Make strong the brick kiln!

—Nahum 3:14 (NKJV)

WE ALL HAVE these obscure moments in our life when someone or something comes along, and we feel like we have hit a brick wall. We seem to hit our head, for whatever reason, against this brick wall until we just can't see straight. After a period of time, we walk away, but not without our own set of bruises, pain, and hurt.

Sometimes this is a person (painful!), sometimes a church (this feels like a knife has been thrust into you), and sometimes it might be family (oh, how crushing this can be). Why, oh, why do we put ourselves through these horrible, terrible, painful situations that will only bring us to the feeling of hitting that brick wall?

With a chronic illness, we hit our own brick wall often enough on our own. We don't need to add any of the above. When I was first diagnosed, my mother and I would go to our local Walmart, which was thirty miles from the home we shared with my grandparents. We were their caregivers. Mom could see in my eyes when I hit my brick wall when we were shopping. She knew I was done and down for the count. Like a fighter, fibro had knocked me down, and the count was over. I've been married since 2010, and Mom can still see in my eyes when I hit my brick wall. My hubs learned quickly about my brick wall.

Most of us have been brought up to have faith in humanity, so we continue to believe in the good of man (and woman). We experience the pain of false friends from early childhood—girls more so than boys. There are some girls that just develop into that "mean girl" attitude easily and carry it on into their adult years, earning the title of strong-willed or strong and heady personality. Oh, just say what you mean. They are mean! Where is their brick wall?

Do you struggle with a brick wall when you do too much? Even all these years later, I can hit my brick wall around the holidays when I take on too much. But I enjoy doing the things I do for my family. Then after everything is done, the families all leave. My hubs puts me to bed so I can rest for days on end. Rebuilding my brick wall once again, piece by piece by piece. I use praise music, scripture, and Southern gospel music for my rebuilding, letting God heal me and speak to me. What will you use?

Pray that you will find where you struggle with your brick wall. Ask God to help you remember that your brick wall will be different than a friend that also hits brick walls when energy is low and the day wears too long. Ask God to give you peace when you hit the wall. Remember, this section is "Remembering that God Is on Your Side." He will not fail you no matter what. Blessings and gentle hugs today, dear friend.

My Yoke Is Easy

For My yoke is easy and My burden is light.

—Matthew 11:30 (NKJV)

WHAT IS WEIGHING you down today? Does pain have a grip on you today? Or fear? Loneliness? Or maybe it is your finances? Could it be that time is fleeting by as you sit at your window, watching the day pass from morning to night, day after day after day after day? Sickness wears you down.

We tend to get caught up in our own selves when we have a long-term illness or disability. We tend to become self-absorbed, especially in the beginning or when we are in a bad flare and, to put it bluntly, our disease sucks. Plain and simple. Sorry for the word, but we really do not have life at its fullest, do we?

After twenty plus years with the disease of fibro, there are multiple diagnosis that have been added to my list. My allergies could take up this entire page and the next. But I can still have periods that get me down. Winter is not my friend. I have no control over the weather. There are other things, however, I can control: my activity level, the foods I eat, avoiding stress. Medications sometimes add to the problems. But there again, you have no control.

I have to remember, "my yoke is easy." But what came before this in the Bible?

> Come to me, all you who are weary and burdened, and I will give you rest. Take My yoke

upon you and learn from Me, for I am gentle and humble in heart, and you will find rest for your souls.

—Matthew 11:28–29 (NIV)

I know some of you are trying to work with your illness. This section of verses should give you hope. Jesus will give you rest. He will give ALL of us rest—rest for our bodies, rest for our souls. Jesus is there for each of us. He wants us to come to Him, to learn from Him, and to rest—to rest.

Pray that you can rest, dear friends. Blessings and gentle hugs.

I Am with You

And He said, "My presence shall go with
you, and I will give you rest."

—Exodus 33:14 (NASB 1995)

I LOVE THE book of Exodus, such a timely story even today—Moses dealing with a stiff-necked people. Are we any different now? Even if we were not facing an illness that has turned our world upside down, searching for diets that would make our lives easier, juggling calendar dates with the numerous doctor's appointments, and taking the medications that leave us with side effects that sometimes seem worse than the illness itself, it is enough to make one weary and wishing for manna from heaven.

"I will give you rest." We all seek it, even when we do not face an illness. Ask any new mother. Remember those days of the 2:00 a.m. feedings, the colic, unending diaper changes, clinging babies, teething, colds, and the sleepless nights that never end? You think, when this tiny one starts to sleep through the night, "I will have rest." Not so. There are new worries, new fears, and they grow as the child grows. All of a sudden, this infant is a toddler getting into everything, then in school, and before you know it, getting a driver's license. Is it any wonder mothers have dark circles under their eyes?

And you think, *When they move out, I can rest.* That's a laugh! A whole new set of worries kick in. You wonder, *Are they eating right? Are they paying their bills? Are they finding the right friends?* And, oh, how you miss having them under your own roof! We are a stiff-necked people, just like those that Moses dealt with.

In Exodus, as Moses communicated with God, He was upset, wanting to know how he (Moses) could know that He (God) was around.

> Now therefore, I pray, if I have found grace in
> Your sight, show me now Your way, that I may
> know You and that I may find grace in Your sight.
> And consider that this nation is Your people.
>
> —Exodus 33:13 (NKJV)

Would we talk to God like this? I should. And we should talk to our kids and family in a way that shows that we are together in reminding them that we need rest.

Take time to rest during the day. Make your bedroom a restful haven. Add candles and extra pillows. Be sure you have lotion and ChapStick, booties, and any other goodies that make you feel loved and comfy. Pray today that you will find your rest. Pray that you will know when to seek grace and when to seek rest. Blessings on you today and gentle hugs, dear friend.

DAY 33

No Excuses

Do all that is in your heart for God is with you.

—1 Chronicles 17:2b (NKJV)

SOMETIMES, WHEN WE get bad news, we just sit and soak it in. Understandable. But then there are times that the sitting takes over and over and over. Get up, people. Time to move!

Do you have a dream? Life is not over just because you have been diagnosed with a chronic illness, making you think that your world has been turned upside down, and Goliath is tromping all over your yard and house. You have to find a way (and the strength) to turn it right again and start over.

I was a social worker. I could not continue in my line of work. Why? We had new laws coming down each day. I could not remember them and compute them into my brain along with the old ones. I could not keep them all straight. I would have such a fibro fog that spelling, the laws, names, dates, addresses—everything—just flew out of the proverbial window. No one could read my writing anymore, including me! I felt lost in the vastness of it all. I was in tears many days. I was limited to the amount of time I could drive. My supervisor suggested I was done. That hurt.

At church, after thirty years of working with children and youth, I no longer had the patience to do so. I struggled to play the piano because my hands would shake so bad. Singing a solo at church became an issue as I couldn't remember the words, and I couldn't hold the microphone. I shook so bad. I froze all the time. I had to wear gloves both at church and the grocery store year-round.

I hit rock bottom. There were cliffs on both sides. I didn't know how I was going to pull myself out of where I was. So what really happened to me? I was put on disability at work, as there was no way I could do my job. And for the first time in over thirty years, I just sat during worship and soaked everything in. I didn't have anything to do. I wasn't teaching anywhere. I wasn't singing. I wasn't having to run here or run there. I was able to just sit and rest and soak in the teaching that was going on. It was a relief. Before I knew it, I noticed a rope ladder on the cliff, and I was climbing up the side slowly. I had to learn to say NO before I could come out of the bottom of the valley.

Pray today that you can do all that is in your heart. Blessings and gentle hugs, dear friend.

DAY 34

Sweet Peace

The Lord lift up His countenance upon you and give you peace.

—Numbers 6:26 (NKJV)

Is THERE A way that you find peace when you are in pain? How do you escape? I pray and hope that it is not medication only but something else. I have been down the road of medication. Then thanks to a misled physician, I had to go through the agony of a terrible withdrawal. I was told by this physician that I would not become addicted to the medications (two of them). Then I was taken off of them, and I was going through withdrawal, cold turkey. It was agony, pure torture. While dealing with this torture, I found a favorite verse:

> Trust in the Lord with all your heart, and lean not on your own understanding; in all your ways acknowledge Him, and He shall direct your paths. Do not be wise in your own eyes, fear the Lord and depart from evil. It will be **health to your flesh** and **strength to your bones**.

—Proverbs 3:5–8 (NKJV) (bold mine)

Verse 8 was my key: health to my flesh and strength to my bones. Wow! I had read these verses for years. I had them memorized. And yet, until now, they were limited in the meaning. Verse 5 and 6 had always been very meaningful: trust in the Lord, lean not, acknowledge Him. I lived my life this way. I tried to make this a daily part of me. But verse 8, health to my flesh and strength to my bones—I thought to myself, *How crazy that I have seen this verse a billion times, and now it makes total sense.* I have returned to this verse time and time again since then. It continues to remind me that I am healed.

Do you have a special verse reminding you that God is on your side? Write it out here.

Now you can return to your verse when you need a reminder that God is on your side.

Remember that God can carry all the burdens. Pray when you think your wagon is too full, God is there for you. Call upon Him. He will give you sweet peace, my dear friend. Blessings and gentle hugs today, my friend.

DAY 35

I Know My Master

Glory and honour are in His presence; strength
and gladness are in His place.

—1 Chronicles 16:27 (KJV)

ONE OF THE definitions of glad (a form of gladness) is "having a cheerful or happy disposition by nature." My rheumatologist has often told me he has a hard time telling what my pain level is because I always have a smile on my face. I am thankful for this. I try to always be someone that maintains a smile. What about you? Can you maintain a smile? My husband and my mother know my pain face, but I try so extremely hard not to show it. Do you keep your pain hidden inside, or do you let the whole world see it? Do you invite everyone to your pity party?

Can you say you are fully empowered by God? We are continuing in the section "Remembering that God Is on Your Side." Glory and honor are in His presence. Strength and gladness are in His place. These are strong words for us. Let's look at each one.

Glory: Praise, honor, renown, distinction, exaltation
Honor: Respect, esteem, recognition, admiration

Each of these words could be put in the verse in place of glory and honor, and the verse would still ring true. In the presence of God, we give Him all praise and respect. We give Him all exaltation and admiration. What do you give Him when you are alone?

Strength: Solidity, toughness, strong, impregna-
    bility
Gladness: Joy, delight, pleasant, happiness

Again, these words can be put in place of those they define in the verse. You can also find other words that define those and replace them. But look at this: "Toughness and delight are in His place." They appear to be polar opposites, yet they are both in place with Him. Why? Because He is Lord of all. He is King of kings. He is the Master of the Wind and the Creator of the universe.

He is there for us, if only we would reach out to Him. He has His arms open wide, as wide as the cross—the cross of Calvary. He still has the nail prints in His hands. How can you say no to Him? He had the strength to go to the cross for you, even if you were the only one that needed Him. He has strength for you when you are in pain, when you are weak, when you are wrapped in sin. He has strength for you when your heart is heavy. Will you accept what He has to offer?

Pray for strength today to turn your frown upside down into a smile. Pray that you will find joy in what you do. Pray that you will find happiness and peace. Blessings and gentle hugs, dear friends.

DAY 36

There's a Fly in My Salad!

In your relationships with one another, have
the same mindset as Christ Jesus.

—Philippians 2:5 (NIV)

IN A LITTLE rural town in Southwest Missouri, on a man-made lake,
I lived with my mother and grandparents. I helped my mother care
for my grandparents. I did this while working full-time, dealing with
my fibro, sometimes caring for one or two of my granddaughters and
volunteering at my local church. Did I have a full and active life? Yes,
I did. Did I suffer a lot from my fibro? Yes, I did. But I also kept it
to myself as much as possible. There were only a very few that knew
I had this disease, and I tried hard to keep it that way. I would not
make extended plans for fear of having to cancel. My doctor said I
was burning the candle at both ends and in the middle. Little did I
know what I was doing to myself.

On a particular Saturday, Mother and I ran some errands and
decided to stop at the marina on the way home for lunch. She was
not a big fan of water yet loved sitting on this houseboat turned
restaurant to eat and watch the boats. We placed our order, getting
our usual from any place—Mom a cheeseburger and me a large salad.
Our meal arrived, and Mom started right in. I gazed at mine, wondering where to start. Then after two bites, I wished I hadn't taken
any at all, for staring up at me was a large dead fly! Mom called the
waitress over as I was tongue-tied. We showed the fly to her, and the
waitress had the audacity to claim that we brought the dead fly in

with us! The waitress then called the manager/chef to come to the table, and he also claimed we brought the fly in with us! We got up a left.

The mindset of Christ allowed us to keep a Christlike presence instead of getting uppity and burly back at the waitress and manager. We just took the high road and got up and left, leaving them both as tongue-tied as I originally had been. As I look back on this time, this is also the kind of fun I could have missed out on had I not been with my mom. She was there as my support and as my sidekick!

Pray that we can laugh at ourselves in the midst of others disregarding our needs. We need to be able to do this from time to time. Blessings and gentle hugs today, dear friend.

One Body

And let the peace of God rule in your hearts, to which
also you were called in one body; and be thankful.

—Colossians 3:15 (NKJV)

I CAN REMEMBER growing up and seeing my mother's hands and thinking they were the most beautiful hands in all the world. I hoped someday that I would have hands as beautiful as hers. Mother's fingers were long and thin. She had veins that popped up and showed through the skin on the top, like a map, as if showing the travels of her life. Oh, if only I thought.

Thanks to my fibro, vitamin deficiencies, playing piano since a child, gardening, and housekeeping; I fuss with my nails a lot. As I was looking at my hands the other day, I thought, *My goodness, you have such thin fingers, and your veins are popping up all over your hands. What ugly hands you've got!* Then it dawned on me that I had my mother's hands. I am thankful for my hands, and I have decided they are beautiful. I will forever have a part of my mother with me no matter what.

I can remember arriving at either of my daughter's homes and little eyes watching out the window for me, waiting for Mema to arrive for a visit. Upon seeing me, arms would wave widely, and smiles of glee would break across faces. Before I could get out of my car, I would hear the joyful immature voices ring out, "Mema's here! Mema's here!" My heartstrings would tighten with joy. Before I could get in the door, arms would be wrapped around my knees, and giggles would erupt around me. Love was in the air. By night-fall, I could be found on the couch, freshly bathed girls snuggled around me with their blankies. Savoring their love and sweetness, giving promises that I would still be there in the morning, I would send them off to bed.

These same girls are young adults and teens now. No longer do they watch out the window for Mema. Instead, it is Mema watching for them. No more snuggles after bath time. I miss those years. They vanished all too quickly. Today I get occasional texts, sometimes a thank-you for a gift.

I find myself seeing a reflection of life in God's eyes through all of this. How we must have looked at Him at first. When we are new Christians, we run to the Bible, we run to prayer, we run to our Lord. But when the years pass, all too often, we wander away from Him. Oh, how He wants us to come home. He has not moved. He is wait-ing and watching for us—for you and for me. Christ loves your knee mail...ouch or rocking chair mail. We are all in one body together, no matter where you are, where I am. Pray today that you will see a reflection of Christ in you as you mature in your walk.

Blessings and gentle hugs today, dear friend.

Railroad Tracks of Time

For all the promises of God in Him are Yes, and in
Him Amen, to the glory of God through us.

—2 Corinthians 1:20 (NKJV)

My DADDY WORKED for the (now defunct) Rock Island Lines Railroad
when I was growing up. He would get guest passes for our family to
take the train from Davenport, Iowa, where we lived into Chicago.
I loved riding the train. I still do. Daddy died on Christmas Day in
1971. I was thirteen.

Every girl needs her daddy. But I still had my Heavenly Father.
He never left my side. And through my young adult years, my
Heavenly Father and I walked side by side. I'm older now. Time has
begun to show it's marching along with me. I am blessed to be in my
early sixties and not have crow's feet yet, however I do have laugh
lines around my mouth and railroad tracks across my forehead.

I don't care. Oh, yes, I do! The train crawls over daily, and sometimes there are boxcars that park right on my forehead (migraine).

Why do we, as individuals worry, about the way we look? We
worry about our weight, the lines and our wrinkles. The clothing we
wear and what we have in our closet. The amount of money we have
(or don't have), and we compare ourselves to family and friends. We
wonder or worry about living in the correct neighborhood, going to
the right church and being seen in the right crowd. Why can we not
be happy with what we have or with what God has blessed us with?

People, we need to make friends with our body!—the fat, the lines, the shapes. We need to make friends with the closet and what we have in there. We need to make friends with our home. We need to be happy with what we have and let God show us the glory of what tomorrow will be in His time. But in all honesty, for most of us, the railroad will run over us and the train of life will chug along, leaving wrinkles and scars where it wants. No matter what the TV tries to sell, we have to realize that the medications we take cause a lot of the lines we see. When we begin to age, the medication doubles or triples those years, causing the lines to take hold. Pray that you will be able to withstand the railroad of time, the lines, scars, and wrinkles. Ask God to help you as life chugs along, leaving its mark. You know nothing you do will erase those years. So make yourself happy when you look in the mirror and say, "Hello, beautiful." God shines through you, dear one.

Blessings and gentle hugs, dear friends.

DAY 39

Your Burning Bush Moment

There the angel of the LORD appeared to him in flames of fire from within a bush. Moses saw that though the bush was on fire it did not burn up. So, Moses thought, "I will go over and see this strange sight—why the bush does not burn up." When the LORD saw that he had gone over to look, God called to him from within the bush, "Moses! Moses!" And Moses said, "Here I am." "Do not come any closer," God said. "Take off your sandals, for the place where you are standing is holy ground."

—Exodus 3:2–5 (NIV)

MOST OF US know the story of Moses standing at the burning bush and talking to God. This was his first encounter with our Lord. He was commanded to take off his sandals, for he was standing on holy ground. For Moses, it was his ah-ha moment. The moment was so strong that Moses's hair and beard turned white because he had been in the presence of God.

Now is the time for our ah-ha moment, to accept the burning bush in our life, our disease and to give it its moment, then carry on. You can live each day to the fullest. You can live life again. Yes, probably with adjustments, but you just need to find what works for you.

Going on vacation? Plan time to rest. Holidays upon you? Delegate, delegate, delegate! And of course, rest. The stress of the holidays, weather, and family will put you into a flare every time if you are not careful. Going through a personal crisis? Rest! Find someone you can trust to share what is going on, and eat well. High protein, low carbs, low sugar work best for most of us with a chronic illness. Avoid aspartame, which is an additive to beverages as a sweetener. Avoid anything with MSG. Watch your sodium, BUT do what your physician tells you to do regarding your diet. I am not trying to advise here. Please understand that!

Pray, asking God to help you make plans so you don't get caught having a bad day and end up without your sandals to carry you across the sand and prepare you for your ah-ha moment. If you are prepared, you will be able to say, "I was ready." If not, the response will be, "So much for that burning bush moment." Blessings and gentle hugs today, dear friend.

DAY 40

True Peace in God

And God will wipe away every tear from their eyes; there
shall be no more death, nor sorrow, nor crying. There shall
be no more pain, for the former things have passed away.

—Revelation 21:4 (NKJV)

I LOVED *THE Hiding Place*[3] by Corrie ten Boom when I was growing
up. (I still do!) As a young adult, I spent a few years in Germany
when my family was in the US Army, and my understanding and
sympathy for what Corrie and her family must have gone through
took on an entirely deeper meaning. As I have grown older and developed the diseases God has blessed me with (yes, blessed me with!), I
have found even more truth in the quotes this dear lady has shared us
with. When she said any of these gems, she had no idea they would
end up as the magnified quotes they are. Look at this one: "If you
look at the world, you'll be distressed. If you look within, you'll be
depressed. If you look at God, you'll be at rest."

How can you be in God's presence and be distressed? Missed
church on Sunday, and your entire week just feels out of connection
and offtrack. How can you look at the world and not be depressed?
Watched the news lately, either local or national? We get mini sound
bites and all it is, is depressing little stories of another shooting, more
flooding, additional fears from our government, pandemic on the rise

---

[3] *The Hiding Place*, written by Corrie ten Boom with John and Elizabeth Sherrill
(Bantam Books, 1971), obtained from the book itself.

again (or is it over), police being murdered or murdering someone in the "line of duty," layoffs by the thousands, millions going bankrupt due to all that is going on in the world. And yet there are weddings being planned and babies being born. Families going on vacations and outings and generally enjoying their lives. Look to God to be at rest. Look to God for your joy and your strength.

This second set of twenty days has been about remembering that God is on your side. God is always on our side. If you have not read Corrie's book, now would be a good time to do so. It would remove you from your self-imposed mirror. Corrie and her sister were subjected to all kinds of horror at the hands of the Nazis. They were the Goliath that these women and many others faced during many dark days. But according to their faith, they stood strong. They knew that God was on their side. They had to experience their Goliath. Are you able to do that, my friend?

Pray today, asking God to help you find your true peace in Him. Blessings and gentle hugs today, dear one.

SECTION 3

Keeping a Stone in Your Pocket

DAY 41

Slingshots and Stones

Then he took his staff in his hand; and he chose for himself
five smooth stones from the brook, and put them in a
shepherd's bag, in a pouch which he had, and his sling
was in his hand, and he drew near to the Philistine.

—1 Samuel 17:40 (NKJV)

FIVE SMOOTH STONES—WE have seen them. Small stones are painted
up so cute to look like a ladybug, a fish, a frog. All sorts of things
show up on these stones, even dice, in case you want to throw them
for a chance at a change in your life.

But I do not think the five smooth stones David picked up had
any cute pictures on them.

We also find stones with sayings on them: joy, hope, love, peace,
or family.

Again, I don't think David found any stones that said, "Kill
him," "Peace," or anything else.

David put his faith in his God. David knew his God would
take the right stone from the bag. David knew it needed to be just
right when he placed it in his sling. He knew God would take care
of the big picture. Why did David know this? And where was that
stone going to land? David knew God was in charge because he stood
on the side of the army of God, not in the uniform that King Saul
tried to load him down with (1 Samuel 17), not surrounded by the
army of the Israelites who were shaking in their sandals. But David
was standing with God, his faith, his sling, and the stones. And how

did David know where that stone would land? Goliath was covered in a huge armor. Standing at a height that he could reach the top of a basketball rim and weighing at over nine hundred pounds, why did he even need the armor when he faced a nation that quaked in their sandals? David looked him over, reached into his bag of stones, pulled out one, and threw the death kill.

So as we enter our last twenty days together, what might your stones say? This section begins a time of joy. Do you have a stone of joy in your garden? Can you look at your disease this way yet? Yes, I know sometimes it can be hard. For me, after the holidays are over, and I have overextended myself in energy, and winter sets in again, I struggle to find my peace and joy with my disease. But I have discovered through the years where I look. But I find ways to heal and find my joy. These are two of my stones, and here is a verse that says it all… a verse we all need to look at.

> Consider it all joy, my brethren, when you encounter various trials, knowing that the testing of your faith produces endurance. And let endurance have its perfect result, that you may be perfect and complete, lacking in nothing.
>
> —James 1:2–4 (NAS)

It says to consider or to count it all joy. **All joy**—the good, the bad, the ugly. Yes, you will still have those bad days. Like I have already mentioned, I do too. But I get my favorite purple blankie, sweet tea, and a couple of my favorite movies that will help bring joy and laughter.

I pray that you can find the time to grow in joy. Pray. Seek God's help to find your smooth stones. Find joy in all circumstances. Blessings and gentle hugs today, dear friend.

====================

DAY 42

====================

Your Season of Choice

Then God said, "Let there be lights in the firmament of
the heavens to divide the day from the night; and let them
be for signs and seasons, and for days and years."

—Genesis 1:14 (NKJV)

WHAT IS YOUR favorite season? Mine is late spring into summer. My
husband would say summer because the warm, sunny days make my
fibro feel soooo much better. However, there are many days in the
summer that a high-pressure system will really bother me. But, oh,
that sweet spring into summer!

Days are getting longer. Grass turns green, and mowers are out.
I love the smell of freshly mowed yards. I know, that's a crazy smell
to love. Trees are turning green again. Flowers are blooming. The sun
is shining, saying hello to the world with a fresh warmth. Birds are
singing a new song of happiness as well.

Then a spring storm arrives, and I am back on my couch with
my blankie. Sometimes it seems I just can't get away from that!

For some, the favorite season is fall. The heat of summer is
over. Fall festivals are just around the corner, and kids are back in
school. (I do not participate in Halloween.) My favorite part of fall
is Thanksgiving. Thanksgiving is a celebration with family and food
but no stockings or presents, no rushing around. It is a blessing in
fall for us all. That is one of the few parts I like about fall. I make
apple butter, and I can from our garden. This is a busy time, and
the days are growing shorter. I hate short days. However, the smells

coming from the kitchen enrich the house, even as the enjoyment of the work wears me out. They are the long-forgotten scents of apple cider, pumpkin pie, chili, anything apple-flavored baking, and cookies baking.

My husband's favorite season is winter. He is very warm natured, and the colder air makes him comfortable. We struggle with the household temperature unless he is sick. Haha. He would be happy with the Christmas tree up all year long! Can you imagine? We can go into any Christmas tree ornament shop and usually pick up one or two items. But the rushing around to get everything done, the meals cooked, the gifts wrapped, stockings hung…Hubs could do without all of that. Why? I am sure it has something to do with the way I overdo.

When we are in our favorite season, how different our mood is then when we are in a season that does not become us. Pray we will not struggle to be nice, to be joyful, to be happy. Ask for an extra touch of strength and endurance during both your favorite season and your worst. Ask God to help make every season your choice. Amen. Remember, rejoice! Put on your big girl/big boy pants, and know that your Goliath has gone down, that you are the winner.

Blessings and gentle hugs, dear friend.

DAY 43

Delight Always

Rejoice in the Lord always. Again I will say, rejoice!

—Philippians 4:4 (NKJV)

How does one show great delight? Rejoice. How does one show awe and amazement? Rejoice. How does one show great happiness? Rejoice. I imagine, for most of us, we picture our family Christmas or a favorite vacation when we think of great delight. I also think of the first time I held my babies and my grandchildren—oh, the delight I had at those moments. (However, the 3:00 a.m. feeding, a few weeks later, took on an entirely different picture!)

I have begun to wonder what delight looks like from the heavenly realm as I have gotten older. I have several family members on the other side, and there are times that I wonder what delights them on the heavenly side—sitting at the feet of Jesus, singing in the heavenly choir, talking with the prophets that have gone before us.

Delight. Rejoice. Look back at how far you have come on day 43 of your journey. You have left the dark side—the unending pain and suffering; the poor, poor, pitiful me attitude. You have turned over a new leaf and decided that there is more to life than your chronic illness. This has happened not only because you have learned a lot about your chronic illness, but you have also come out of the shell of your life and moved on. You have realized that God's presence is there with you. You have a new lease on life in God. You know that you can dance in the showers of blessings with God at your side.

According to BibleGateway.com online, there are 238 verses that contain the word *rejoice* in it. Broken down, this is 179 in the Old Testament and 59 in the New Testament. Psalms contain the most with 60 verses, and numerous books have only 1 verse.

> Serve the Lord with fear, and rejoice with trembling.
>
> —Psalm 2:11 (NKJV)

> You defend them; let those also who love Your name be joyful in You.
>
> —Psalm 5:11c (NKJV)

> I will be glad and rejoice in You; I will sing praise to Your name, O Most High.
>
> —Psalm 9:2 (NKJV)

Pray, asking God to guide you as you find verses on rejoicing and delight that will hold a special meaning for you. Ask God to help you sing to your heart's content if your verse is from a praise chorus. Even if you cannot carry a tune, no one cares as you are singing to God.

Rejoice, joy, delight—find your stones and paint them. Delight today, dear friend. May your day be filled with numerous smiles. Blessings and gentle hugs, dear friends.

A Look in the Mirror

Let the words of my mouth and the meditation of my heart Be acceptable in Your sight, O Lord, My strength and My redeemer.

—Psalm 19:14 (NKJV)

I LOOK IN the mirror, and I see two faces. I see the face of who I long to be, and I see the face of who I am. One is the face of pain and exhaustion. The other face I see is someone trying to put on a show, a mime of "I am okay," "I do not hurt," "I can make it through another day," "I can do this. Yes, I can." Oh, if only I could go back to the point that caused the fibro and fix it. But we all dream, don't we? We all have our "if onlys" sometimes.

So how on earth do we carry through? How can we make it through another day of pretending, of putting on a face that is a smile when everything might not be right, but we want it to be? Where is that stone of peace, that stone of joy? We are on day 44 of our sixty-day walk, and this section is about joy. Can you count your days of joy? Did you start that joy/blessing jar? Attitude is everything as we carry on, carry over, and carry through. Many physicians might suggest you try things like biofeedback, aromatherapy, music, massage, guided imagery, self-hypnosis, and acupuncture. Of course, nowhere does prayer, scripture reading, and devotionals appear on the therapies a physician might suggest.

So where does your search lead you for some extra pain control? As long as you do not lose sight of your Heavenly Healer, it is okay to use some of these therapies. A wonderful hot bath with scented candles and low music playing in the background can be very soothing. (Just be sure to keep candles and music a safe distance from your tub!) Massage if you can handle that. But for me, I cannot. I don't handle this well! I have tried acupuncture (at a chiropractor's clinic) and discovered no relief. Each person must try what they are led to and see what works for them. Anything that does not hurt your body, does not lead you astray, is not dangerous, unlawful, or illegal is acceptable and fair game. Again, just check with your doctor!

Make friends with yourself. Make friends with your body. Make friends with you. Pray today seeking God's reflection as you look in the mirror and see your happy self. Blessings and gentle hugs, dear friend.

DAY 45

Fill Me Up, Lord

Jesus answered and said to her, "Whoever drinks of this water will
thirst again, but whoever drinks of the water that I shall give him
will never thirst. But the water that I shall give him will become
in him a fountain of water springing up into everlasting life."

—John 4:13–14 (NKJV)

I WATCHED A commercial on TV today (something I do not usually
do) to a tune by John Denver. There were no words. Nothing was
being sold. There was no pushy "clean up" this or that. It was just
scenes of America rolling by that tied into the song. It was beautiful.
No post-it at the bottom when the song ended that said, "brought to
you by" this car or that hotel or some insurance. It just said, "America,
come home again." Fresh. New. Engaging.

It brings to mind another song, "How Great Thou Art,"[4] and
it has to make one think on the things of God. On this particular
day, I am making apple butter. It is fall, and this is just something
that I have to do in the fall. The goodness of God is captured in an
apple, shown in the trees as they turn red, yellow, purple, and gold.
The heat of summer is fading to cool nights and softer days. There is

---

4   "How Great Thou Art," words and music by Carl Boberg; words were translated
from Swedish into English by Stuart K Hine. It was originally written in 1885,
and the English translation was completed in 1949. There were other English
translations before and after 1949; however, they did not contain all the "verses"
that the original poem contained (Google Internet services).

something refreshing about fall before the dreary days of winter set in. And God, in all His glory, set His palette on glorious colors.

What season are you in? Maybe it is spring, and tulips are pushing their way up through the tired winter-weary earth. Life anew is coming to your area. We have already talked about your favorite season, but as spring brings a new life to your community, there are little buds bursting out on the trees. Winter hibernation is over. Are you returning to a new energy and new zeal for life? Maybe it is summer, and you are basking in the sun, drinking lemonade, and watching your garden grow. Ants are busy with their picnic work as you are out in the sun. Ah, the joys of summer!—heat, picnics, walks, and sunsets that are painted by God Himself, paintings that would rival anything in the Louver or the Vatican. Butterflies and hummingbirds dance around trees and flowers, taking and giving life.

Or maybe you are in the winter season. This season, many of us dread. But there is joy here, if only we would look. We have to look beyond Christmas and the carols. Watching it snow while being all snug inside is delightful. Add a fire in your fireplace, a cup of hot chocolate or hot cider, and you are doing well. If you don't have a fireplace, there are plenty of electric fireplaces that are attractive and can become a useful piece of furniture that actually puts out heat. We had two of these, one in our home and the other in our RV. I keep telling myself that winter is only eight weeks long, just two months. If I can get through January and February, I have it made! The best thing to remember about this season is the birth of our Lord. He fills our lives, no matter what.

Pray today. Ask God to complete you in whatever season you are in. Ask God to give you praise, no matter where you are. Ask God to show you a palette of colors and beauty, no matter what awaits you outside your window today. Blessings and gentle hugs, dear friend, blessings.

DAY 46

My Strength and My Song

The Lord is my strength and my shield; my heart trusted
in Him, and I am helped; therefore my heart greatly
rejoices, and with my song I will praise Him.

—Psalm 28:7 (NKJV)

"It Is Well with My Soul"[5]—this is not only one of my favorite hymns to sing but probably my life song. I will find myself humming and singing this both when I am down and when I am happy. This hymn was an anchor for my soul when my middle daughter was ill, when I was suffering from a marriage of abuse, when I was learning to live with the fibro and all the additional diagnoses. This was my hymn when my oldest granddaughter ran away from home and my third oldest granddaughter had some struggles that same year. Life is full of difficulties, and this is my go-to hymn.

Oh, how the Lord speaks to us when we are in Him. Oh, how sweet is the unity when we are in that sweet, sweet spirit that is part of the living Word that is our Lord. He, and He alone, is the Rock of our salvation.

Rejoice in your strength. Do you know who your strength is? Where does it come from? Are you feeling a renewal of your health and life yet? You may not have a newfound control of your medications, diet (if there is one), and life, but give it time. Forty-seven days

---

5 "It Is Well with My Soul," written by Horatio G. Spafford in 1873, music by Phillip P. Bliss in 1876 (Wikipedia).

is not enough time to learn all you need for a life change. Remember, it will come, but you have made a great start. Forty-seven days is not enough time for those of us that are "lifers" with our chronic illness, as we can suddenly be hit with that "train of despair" out of nowhere that tells us something is not right. When we have overdone once again, and all we have done is gone grocery shopping or prepared dinner and cleaned up the dishes. Our illnesses are strange and demanding things that will knock us for a loop at any given time.

Yes, you have had some ups and downs, and some downs and up. Then there have been the loop-de-loops, just like you were on a roller coaster. You will have more of those days and weeks… that is a guarantee. Just remember this, Jesus is the source of your strength. He is your shield of protection. You will be able to rejoice as you get stronger each and every day. Keep your eyes ahead of you so you are not surprised at what comes your way, and all will be well with your soul.

Pray. Ask God to give you your strength and your song. Ask God to give you the joy to rejoice each day as you sing, praise, and dance. God is your strength and your Redeemer. His shield will protect you. You are His child, and He is yours! Blessings and gentle hugs today, dear friend.

DAY 47

Footprints of the Savior

The Lord God is my strength; He will make my feet like
deer's feet, and He will make me walk on my high hills.

—Habakkuk 3:19 (NKJV)

THIS BEAUTIFUL YET often missed verse is the basis for the allegorical
novel *Hinds' Feet on High Places*.[6] If you have never read this delightful little book, I challenge you to do so. It is about a young woman
named Much Afraid and her journey away from her family and into
the high places of the Shepherd. She is guided by two companions,
Sorrow and Suffering. (Sounds like the life of those of us with a
chronic illness?) This allegory is about the Christian life and shows
the transformation from unbeliever to salvation through maturity. So
why bring it up here?

Well, because of those two characters in the book, Sorrow and
Suffering. Oh... Sorrow and Suffering...many people continue to
walk with these two, even after they become Christians. Why would
you want to continue to walk with these two? Even without reading this, I imagine you can think what Sorrow and Suffering bring
to Much Afraid's life. What would they bring to your life? Misery?
Exhaustion from the constant drudgery? Bitterness and anger that
develops from the heavy yoke? That heavy yoke, we do not have to
carry. Oh, the agony and hardships that Much Afraid did not have

---

[6] *Hinds' Feet on High Places*, written by Hannah Hurnard in 1955 (Christian
Literature Crusade Publishing).

to endure. What about you? Who have you been walking with? Even if you are a mature Christian, this allegorical book, this story, can be an eye-opener.

Meet the Shepherd. See how gentle He is. Watch as He guides, loves, and meets the needs of Much Afraid. He does the same for us…for you and for me.

> For you were like sheep going astray, but have now returned to the Shepherd and Overseer of your souls.
>
> —1 Peter 2:25 (NKJV)

There are times that I am just like Much Afraid. I have had fibro for well over twenty years now, and yet that is not what will paralyze me with fear. I can stand at the top of an escalator, and I fear that my right leg, the leg that I broke, will fail me. I have tried to get on one over and over and over again. Each time, I have to turn around and find the elevator. I have never been frozen with fear before. This frustrates me, making me feel like I am trapped. I know that I have the Shepherd, yet like Much Afraid, I just cannot take those steps. Each of us must continue to climb, no matter what paralyzes us. We must find the strength to go on.

Pray. Ask God's goodness and grace on this day, and ask for His help when you become Much Afraid. Ask God for His guidance when you become afraid to face the day-to-day things in life. Ask God to help you when Sorrow and Suffering are trying to snuff out the joy in your life and snuff you out. Ask God to keep you in His fold, for you are His sheep, and He is your Shepherd. Blessings and gentle hugs, dear friend.

DAY 48

Two Steps Backward

Jesus wept.

—John 11:35 (NKJV)

YOU MAY WONDER why I saved this verse for this close to the end of our time together. And you may think this verse has nothing to do with chronic illnesses, afflictions, or asking our Lord for release from pain. By now, you probably have an understanding (although limited, if your condition is new) of what you are dealing with. You also are getting a handle on your medications, and the fact that your doctors are going to be changing them often. So why, you wonder, is this devotion here and not closer to the beginning?

Jesus got a message that His dear friend was sick and dying. Jesus could have gone immediately to the town of Bethany, where His friend Lazarus lived with his two sisters, Mary and Martha. He chose instead to wait three days to show His friends, the family, and the world a miracle. But when Jesus arrived in Bethany, first He wept over the loss of His friend and the pain that the family was enduring. He wept over the unbelief of His friends and associates. He wept over what was awaiting Him in just a very short while. Then Jesus stood outside the tomb of Lazarus and commanded him to come forth from the tomb. Do you know what happened? This dead man got up and walked out of his tomb! He was alive at the voice of the Savior!

Within just a few short weeks, Jesus would be walking toward Jerusalem to be met by thousands of His followers. Palm branches were waved for Him and laid down for Him. Jesus wept for that because He knew this was the beginning of the end of His earthly time. But we know that this time was only the beginning of the true beginning! That is why, this verse is here toward the end of our time together because you are going to have a really bad day after you get things figured out, no matter if this is a new condition or if you have been dealing with this for twenty years. You will wake up, one morning, feeling like you have been run over by a semitruck and knowing that it went too fast to get the license plate number. You will try all your usual tricks, and nothing helps. Then the tears will fall and fall and fall. You will feel like a failure, wondering what you have done wrong.

Wipe your tears, my dear friend. Remember, Jesus wept. He wept for you. He knew that you would hurt. He knew that you would have pain. He knew that you would need Him. He knew that you would come to Him at your lowest when all was lost. Jesus wept, and you can too.

Pray. Ask God to give you a new strength, not only today but also for tomorrow. Ask God to wipe away your tears, calm your fears, and give you peace. May you be a blessing to someone today, dear friend. Blessings and gentle hugs to you today.

DAY 49

A Vessel of Use

But may the God of all grace, who called us to His
eternal glory by Christ Jesus, after you have suffered
awhile, perfect, establish, strengthen and settle you.

—1 Peter 5:10 (NKJV)

DON'T YOU JUST love this verse? Let's look at it again: suffered awhile, perfect, establish, strengthen, and settle you! It will be provided by the God of grace who called us to His eternal glory! I don't know about you, but this verse gives me hope and joy.

"Suffered awhile"—I do believe Jesus taught His very own disciples that He would suffer many things. We have already read some of this. Jesus was rejected by His own. He was manhandled. He was tormented. How could this be part of His earthly glory? Could we find meaning in what we have suffered or are currently suffering? Why should we find glory in this? Well, let me share something with you.

Those that live a life with no pain, no suffering, no sorrow cannot witness to someone that walks through those valleys with the same effectiveness as someone that has. As a woman that has suffered at the hands of an abuser in my marriage, I can usually read the marks in a department store or the grocery store of one trying to hide her feelings of failure and abuse. I have been known to try to reach out to these women at times. As a woman that has buried a child, I can understand the pain of a mother that has had to bury her child and know what she needs. As a mother of a prodigal child, I can lead the mother that is suffering that sorrow to moments of clarity, even if she doesn't leave the valley. At least she can be aware that her child didn't become a prodigal because of her. As a woman that has helped care for her parents and grandparents, I can understand those that are serving their families in this way. As a woman that has walked through these kinds of valleys, I have become a better vessel for Christ to use in His kingdom work. I suffered during the pain, but He perfected me for His use. He established me for the work He called me to. He gives me strength when I would feel too weak to go on. When we are walking in Him, He settles our fears and calms our nerves.

What is God calling you to do? Do you need to overcome this Goliath for your service? Are your fears causing your feet to be mired in the clay of doubt? God is not the God of doubt or fear. Fear is Satan's attack, his MO if you will.

Look up at the verse again. Perfect. Establish. Strengthen. Settle.

Yes, you are! You have overcome your doubt and fear. You have overcome your Goliath. You have a new boldness. You have a new strength. Enjoy life. Enjoy the perfection. Pray. Ask God's peace in your life as He continues to guide you to be the perfect vessel you are. Blessings and gentle hugs today, dear friend.

DAY 50

A Lifeline

Pray without ceasing.

—1 Thessalonians 5:17 (KJV)

I REMEMBER WHEN my girls were growing up, I could spend hours in prayer without my mind wandering. I could stay focused and on top of what I was praying about. On my knees, or lying flat on the floor, it made no difference. But these days? It seems like I am a toddler of the prayer class. My mind will wander. My legs will begin to shake and twitch. My body will start to misbehave after just a few moments, causing me to lose focus. I will twitch, turn, and shake until, suddenly, I am no longer praying, and I forget when I stopped or what I was in the middle of praying for. My lifeline is gone. It's like I have hung up on my call to Christ and heaven. So how can I ask you to pray each day when I struggle so myself?

We must find what works the best for ourselves—the best time. Of course, we are told to pray always so you can have a long-running conversation with God each day. Pray without ceasing, without stopping, no matter what we are doing: driving, watching TV, eating, resting, socializing, working. It does not matter. Verse upon verse talks to us about consistent prayer. See if you can find one, and write it out here.

One that I marked in my Bible is, *"in all my prayers for all of you, I always pray with joy" Philippians 1:4. (NIV).* One last thought about prayer: It is a conversation with our Lord. He hungers to hear from you, His child. All it takes is a simple start, so just begin. For me, I now have to write my prayers down. I have over ten prayer journals thus far. These help me to stay focused. I jot down a prayer throughout the day, and this also allows me to go back and see the answers that God has blessed me with. Yes, I may not be physically healed. That apparently is not God's plan. That is okay. Maybe I am a vessel just as I am. So my prayer life shows this, and I have to live this.

How did the Lord teach us to start our prayers? *"Our Father who art in heaven…" Matthew 6:9a (NAS).*

Pray today that you can begin to connect your lifeline. There is no long-distance charge. There is no Internet charge. You will not be disconnected. No Wi-Fi hookup is needed. But a nice journal just might be the one item you do need. It will help you stay focused and beat down the Goliath of missing your prayer time. Blessings on you and your prayer life, dear friend. Blessings and gentle hugs today.

New Adventures, New Challenges

Be of good courage, and He shall strengthen your
heart, all you who hope in the Lord.

—Psalm 31:24 (NKJV)

Do you have a secret heart's desire, some kind of adventure that you would just love to try, but you fear that your illness/disability makes it too difficult for you? Sounds like you are afraid to get in the garden with the jolly green Goliath. So you just stay home and do nothing. You don't try. For a long time, I was a member of the "Stay Home and Hide Club."

I am sure there are many of us that can say we are members of the SHH Club even though no monetary dues were paid. But there have been other dues paid. We have been losing out on family adventures. We have paid by losing out on fun and laughter with our spouse. We have paid by missing out on sunshine and exercise. We have paid by missing the experience of joy, exhilaration, and the thrill of accomplishment. We have paid, paid, paid. And I, for one, am tired of paying the dues to be a member of the SHH Club. I am ready to get off the couch, out of the living room, and head outside for some excitement. How about you?

Today, you will need a pencil and a few moments to think. I have a bucket list of things I want to accomplish and places I want to go while I am able. I am going to share some of them here. Then I want you to dream. Nothing is impossible! Once you have a list of what you want to do, show your Physician. Always get permission from your Physician before trying anything. A little research will show you that even if you are wheelchair bound that there are no obstacles. Even waterparks now have slides made just for you. Dream, look, go, enjoy, and rejoice in what God allows you to do. Knock down your Goliath!

My bucket list:

- Explore the complete Route 66 with my husband
- Tour the Black Hills
- Explore the Smithsonian
- Go see Noah's ark
- Take an Alaskan cruise
- Fly in a hot-air balloon

Now it is your turn. In the space below, list four to six activities or adventures that you would like to do, not something that has to be done today. But dream. This is your chance to leave the SHH Club behind and join a new club—the Adventurers.

Pray today. Ask God to give you the strength to rise up each morning with adventure in you. May you find delight in your day so you can rest in the night. Ask God to bring you dreams of enjoyment. Blessings and gentle hugs today, dear friend.

New Healings

In my Father's house are many mansions: if it were not so.
I would have told you. I go to prepare a place for you.

—John 14:2 (NKJV)

IT IS 3:00 a.m. as I write this, thunderstorms all around. I have decided it is easier to get up then try to discern between hub's snores and the thunder while I watch the lightening streak the skies. And then I get to listen to the squirrels in the attic play run and hide. Yes, we have squirrels in our attic, part of the joy of living in a red cedar home. We often listen to them, as well as woodpeckers pillaging for bugs in the framework.

For those of us living with any chronic illness, the weather oftentimes affects us. A storm such as this will have us up. Many of us are walking the floor a day or two before it even arrives. Some of us are wishing we could soak in a hot tub to help ease the pains. Oh, the aches of this earthly body. We have to remember that every night is holding back a new tomorrow, a fresh day, and a sunrise that will bring a bright horizon for us. We will see the new world, washed in the glory that only God can accomplish when He brings the rains. There may not be a rainbow, but the newness of a fresh day will bring the new tomorrow.

If you suffer from restless leg, you know the plight that this pain can cause in both the daytime and the evenings. Mine hits just before going to bed. Hub's is in the afternoon and evening. I do not know why this disease is not an aerobic activity. It can have your legs going faster than the beaters on your momma's mixer, making Thanksgiving mashed potatoes for hours on end. Why I do not have the legs of a super model after twenty years of this crippling disease. I do not know. But I take a shower, use heating pads, and take my meds to try to keep my legs calm—tears sometimes, God all the time.

As for me and my house, we will serve the Lord.

—Joshua 24:15c (NKJV)

Are you living each day to your fullest? Are you enjoying each day to the best of your ability? I have found that I love the adult coloring books. Sometimes they are very calming for me. I have many of those days in winter that these books come in handy. You don't even have to be an artist to enjoy these books. They are for the young and old alike. I have come to enjoy coloring as you can only watch so much TV. Some, I have discovered, even encourage you to play praise music to enhance your coloring time. It's a wonderful way to have a time of worship when otherwise you might not be able to have one.

Oh, dear friend, as we near the end of our sixty-day journey, please pray today that God would calm you heart when the pain continues to raise its ugly head, as it sometimes will. Ask God to help you keep your eyes focused. Ask Him to help you find a way to praise Him when you do not feel like it. And above all, ask God to prepare a mansion for you. Ask Him into your heart today if you have not already done that. He will cleanse you and prepare you for that mansion. He may not heal (as we have already talked about), but He will walk beside you the rest of the days you walk on this earth, and He will give you rest. Blessings and gentle hugs today, dear friend.

DAY 53

Sufficient Grace

And He said to me, "My grace it sufficient for you, for My strength
is made perfect in weakness." Therefore most gladly I will rather
boast in my infirmities, that the power of Christ may rest upon me.

—2 Corinthians 12:9 (NKJV)

OH, HOW WE fight and grumble when we have a disease. We sit
and play the "if only" card, like it's the only card in our deck. Years
come and go, and no matter what, we still struggle to wrap our heads
around what we cannot do sometimes. We have to stop that. We
have to let go.

Let go of the things we have talked about, and let this be a
gentle reminder. Let go of made beds every day if you need to. Make
them when company comes. Does it really matter? Let go of doing
spring cleaning. Does anyone even do that anymore? Does it really
matter? If you do it, spread it out so you do not do it all in one week,
or ask for help. Let go of being the hero at Christmas. Who said it
had to be done the way it always has been. (This one is my downfall!)
Yes, you would like to keep up certain traditions, but get family to
help. It's time they started to carry them on. Some things you just
can't do without making yourself sick, so pass the torch.

Growing a garden? Make it smaller so that you are not overwhelmed with the produce. I love to can. We had a small garden this
year, and I did can but only a small amount. I had help from Hubs
and even a granddaughter (who has since sworn off tomatoes). If you

don't want the upkeep of a garden but want to can produce, support your local farmer's market.

Another look at our verse: "*My grace is sufficient. You are made perfect in weakness.*" You and I can be made perfect, just as we are in the grace of God's love, the grace of God's perfection, the grace of God. Oh, what better perfection is there? We no longer have to do it all. We can rest when we need to. We can let go of all the things we think we have to get done. We can let go of the earthly perfection that we think we have to have. We can use electric carts at stores and parks. We can hire someone to dust, clean, and vacuum.

Pray today, dear friend, that you no longer see the infirmities that weigh you down. Pray that you no longer seek the earthly perfection that may haunt you. Seek instead the grace of God. Oh, dear one, rejoice in God. And again, I say, rejoice. Blessings and gentle hugs as you rejoice in your newfound freedom.

DAY 54

Faith in Our Wings

But those who wait upon the Lord shall renew their strength;
They shall mount up with wings like eagles, They shall
run and not be weary, They shall walk and not faint.

—Isaiah 40:31 (NKJV)

I WAS SITTING on the front porch of our new home in the swing, watching the various birds fly from tree to tree. It reminded me of the birds I used to watch when I would sit on the deck of our red cedar home, watching the numerous birds high up in the trees. It doesn't matter if the branch is so small that it looks like a single leaf would cause it to bow and break; the bird, anything from an eagle or large hawk to a wee sparrow or blue bird, will rest upon it. They will perch on this branch, which is at the top of a tree, without fear that it will give away on them. And suddenly, it dawned on me why these birds could sit there. These birds have faith in their wings, not in the branch.

There are days when we are stuck on the edge of our own branch. We need to bear in mind that we will not be forgotten if we remain in Christ Jesus. He is the one we have our faith in. He will keep us, no matter where we are perched on our very own branch.

What branch are you sitting on today? Are you hiding on a low branch that is thick and has some coverage to it so you can hide, or are you sitting on a high branch so you can get a grand view of what is around you?

Why have you chosen this branch?

This section is titled "Keeping a Stone in Your Pocket." We've talked about the slingshot and stone that hit Goliath, looking in the mirror, taking two steps backward, using our lifeline. Now, though, is the time to wait upon the Lord, to renew our strength, to run and not be weary.

Pray. Ask God to help you mount up on the branch of your choice, strong like the eagles. Blessings and gentle hugs today, dear friend.

DAY 55

Be Still

Be still and know that I am God.

—Psalm 46:10a (NKJV)

MY HUBS RECENTLY had surgery for cancer. I sat looking at him one day and noticed that he appeared to be on Mars. I asked where he was and what he was thinking about, and he said, "Nothing." What amazes me the most is that this is probably true!

Men have a "nothing" file! I have read this over and over again. Women do not. How on earth can they do this? I try to do nothing, and a million things jump into my head, and they are things that I must complete. My to-do list grows longer and longer. Depending on the season, the list seems to multiply overnight, and sometimes by the hour.

Be Still…

This was so difficult when my children were babies. I will be honest, I thought, *Oh, this will get easier when they grow up*. That has not happened. They became teenagers, and there was a new set of rules and mother issues! Then the grandbabies started to arrive. There have been good times, bad times, busy times, sorrowful times, and joy-filled times. There are those I can't get enough of those grand's times. Why can I not ever find the "just sit back and stay still" times?

According to *Webster's Dictionary*, *still* means "not moving, quiet, subdued, calm, and tranquil." To come into the presence of the Lord in this manner allows us to truly hear what HE wants us to hear. If we had an empty box, suitcase, or file cabinet, we could sit and be still for personal worship in the Lord and then fill it with all He has taught us, to feel His presence and to know Him. We must learn to find our holy closet of worship and prayer. How are we never taught this?

I think this has something to do with our grandmothers. I say this not to be mean, but I know that my grandmothers were never still. From sunup until they went to bed, the only time they stopped was when they sat down to eat or use the privy. I remember my paternal grandmother saying, "A busy woman is a gift from God." I do not know where she got this, but she lived by this until her passing at the age of ninety-one. She made ALL her own clothing, brushed her teeth with baking soda, and had never cut her hair. She believed she was to be busy all the time to be an honorable woman of God. We just need to BE STILL.

Today, pray that you might find the time to be still before and in the Lord. Ask for His strength to help you overcome your Goliath. Ask the Lord for time to get to know Him—be it in song, praise, study, or continued prayer. But "*be still.*" Blessings and gentle hugs today, dear friend.

The Comfort of Old

Yet I will rejoice in the Lord, I will joy in the God of my salvation.

—Habakkuk 3:18 (NKJV)

DO YOU REMEMBER the "good ole days" when you would receive the Christmas gifts of a new doll, bike, skates, a new book, truck, or other toy? How wonderful the feeling was of "the new." The item would go outside to be shown off. New clothes would be worn to church and to school at the first opportunity.

Other "good ole days" are the TV shows that showed only on the three available channels. These are definitely available now but only through the multitude of cable companies, DVDs, and other video avenues. They were clean, easy to watch, and family friendly. In the summer, we could drink out of the garden hose and not worry about it. We could play outside until the streetlights came on without any worries. We would go on family picnics, church picnics, and life was basically very good. It was like catching lightning bugs in a jar. I don't even see lightning bugs much anymore.

But the new became old. The bike lays against the back of the garage wall. The skates hang from a nail in the basement. Toys were put in a box in the attic. "Old and comfortable" is a favorite friend.

Music can be that way. We find in worship many varieties of music these days: hymns, contemporary, Western, Southern gospel, traditional, mixed. I could go on, but many of you probably know what I am talking about. You may wonder why we need so many different styles of music but with so many different people. I think you get the idea. Some of us are familiar with the contemporary music of today. This style has been around since the mid-1980s. However, when you are hurting, you want to go back to the days of old, to the comfort, just like the favorite toys of your childhood, just like your favorite blankie, just like the soft, easy clothes your body craves. So your spirit craves the songs of comfort and days of old. My hubs and I are of two groups. He loves contemporary, and I love Southern gospel and traditional. Give me a good ole hymn, and I go back to my childhood.

When all else fails, find the comfort of your youth. Pray that you can find the songs that will bring you joy and comfort during all your days. That way, when you have days of pain, you will know your go-to songs. Blessings, sweet music, and gentle hugs, dear friend.

DAY 57

The Hidden Losses

Rejoice always, pray without ceasing, in everything give
thanks; for this is the will of God in Christ Jesus for you.

—1 Thessalonians 5:16–18 (NKJV)

ACCORDING TO THE CDC, six in ten adults have a chronic illness, and four in ten have two or more. What are we doing, folks? With over 5 million individuals afflicted with fibro, according to the National Institute of Arthritis and Musculoskeletal Diseases, 34.2 million suffer with diabetes. An overwhelming 6.2 million Americans have Alzheimer's disease. One in over 100,000 afflicted with pseudotumor cerebri. Thirty-seven million individuals have chronic kidney disease. This disease can lead to the loss of the use of your kidneys and the need for dialysis. And migraines—let's not forget how debilitating these can be. Also, according to the CDC, women are twice as likely than men to have migraines. Migraines are considered to be three or more debilitating headaches a month. The last survey that was completed for individuals with migraines was in 1992 (National Institute of Headaches) by the CDC. This survey showed that migraines have increased from 25.8 percent to 36.7 percent per 1,000 population. Just imagine, if you live in a town of 10,000, 3,750 people would suffer from migraines. Many of these chronic illnesses also lead to high blood pressure, heart disease, stroke. The losses to self and family are overwhelming.

But why look at the Goliaths in this world and in your life? Have we not spent almost sixty days, ready to overcome Goliath and slay him? Rejoice always! Give thanks!

Today we have a twofold lesson. First, get some paints or markers and five flat rocks. Then get ready to make your own David stones, whether it is pictures or words. Remember our study on day 41 ("Slingshots and Stones")? Go back if you need to. Think about what you want on your rocks. After you paint, you can seal them so they stay shiny, and the rains don't wash anything away. I pray your words might be *strong*, *fearless*, *joy*, and others like that. Pictures could include a shield. Christ gives us a shield of protection.

> Stand therefore, having girded your waist with truth having put on the breastplate of righteousness, and having shod your feet with the preparation of the gospel of peace; above all, taking the **shield of faith** with which you will be able to quench all the fiery darts of the wicked one. And take the helmet of salvation, and the sword of the Spirit, which is the word of God.
>
> —Ephesians 6:14–17 (NKJV)
> (underline and bold print is mine for emphasis.)

The second part of our lesson today is to just let go. Let go of all that you are hanging on to—the need to ALWAYS be the best, the need to teach every class at church, the need to show up all the time, the need to cook for every occasion, the need to dust, vacuum, do the dishes every night (use your dishwasher folks!), cook a seven-course dinner every night. Just give it up. Say that with me: "Just give it up." One more time. "JUST GIVE IT UP!" Now, can you live by that? I have to say that I have learned to. I have a blessing and a curse in that I am a perfectionist, but I found a sign at a popular decorating store that says, "Forgive the mess, but we live here." Some days, it just kind of says it all. Other days, things are pretty good. I have teenage granddaughters that always need money. Guess what I do? You bet! I hire those gals to dust, sweep away the cobwebs, vacuum, hoe the garden, whatever we need, then we head to the lake.

Back to our verse for the day… Are you able to rejoice now? We are in the season of rejoicing as we near the end. Father, I pray that I will be able rejoice always. That you will help me rejoice when I lose my sight. Help me rejoice always. Help me to rejoice for you are able. Rejoice on the days you feel good. Rejoice on the days you struggle, because you have your comfort items near you. Rejoice that you have strength in Christ Jesus. Today I challenge you to pray that you can always rejoice, that you can wake up with a smile and joy in your heart, that you can be happy with how far you have come with the discoveries about yourself. Blessings and gentle hugs today, dear friend.

Wind and Wings

Because You have been my help, therefore in
the shadow of Your wing I will rejoice.

—Psalm 63:7 (NKJV)

MANY YEARS AGO, there was a movie about two young girls from different worlds that met and became friends. They were friends through their adult years—the ups and downs, the valleys and mountains, the pitfalls and joys. They eventually went their separate ways, as friends oftentimes do. But when cancer came into the picture, a phone call was made, and the friends reunited until the end.

My mother lives in the same area where she went to high school. She sometimes sees friends from school. It amazes me that at eighty-five, she has contact with these individuals. Although the town was and still is less than six hundred, her graduating class was somewhere around ten individuals. (Mom doesn't remember any more.) I however came from a graduating class of over seven hundred, and over twenty years later, I am no longer in contact with any of those individuals. They have all gone their separate ways.

Some of these people found their wings; others found the wind. Some have struggled and are in the pitfall of life; some have passed away, causing me anguish that I did not reach them with the gospel and the truth of Jesus Christ.

My middle daughter died of brain cancer at the age of twenty-one. It had metastasized to her spine, her liver, and throughout her precious body. She was a fighter for four years before the wings of heaven carried her home, where she found her healing. Jesus is more than the wind beneath our wings. We don't have to rely on our own strength if we live in Him. You don't have to rely on anyone else for your strength either, for you have the one true God. He is your ultimate power source.

Pray today that you will know the wings of heaven, the wind of grace, and the power of Jesus Christ. Pray today that you do not let any of your friends or family be left behind. Blessings and gentle hugs today, dear friend.

DAY 59

Clay Vessels

But we have this treasure in earthen vessels, that the
excellence of the power may be of God and not of us.

—2 Corinthians 4:7 (NKJV)

WE HAVE THIS perception that we are strong some days and weak
other days. I beg to find a flaw in this. Because folks, when we are
fighting a chronic illness, like we are, we are strong every day! I
remember, many years ago, when there was a rare but fascinating
find in the Holy Lands of numerous clay pots that held some of the
Dead Sea Scrolls. Oh, to have been a part of that discovery!

Clay vessels were used for thousands of years to hold what
was precious. Fragile? Yes. Just like anyone with a chronic illness.
Sometimes we just want to curl up and climb into our comfort spot,
just like a kitten does into anything tight and soft. Clay vessels of
old held salt for healing. Myrrh, an expensive spice used for making
perfume, medicine, and anointing the dead. It was also used for trade
in Arabia, Abyssinia, and India. It was said to have been made for
kings. Any wonder it was brought by the wise men to the manger of
our Savior?

Women kept oil in their earthly jars for cooking, for lighting
the lamps in the evening, and for anointing our Lord. Salt was kept
in clap pots as it was used for curing meats, healing wounds (ouch!
maybe this is where the saying "rubbing salt in a wound" came
from?), and sometimes for trading.

You see, clay vessels or pots were known to have great value. And you, my friend, are no different. You are a vessel of great worth. As we approach the last day, I want you to realize this. I want you to express yourself by writing down the worth and joy you have in yourself. This is not bragging; this is knowing that you are OKAY, and your illness is not winning! Take a few moments, and write down how God is helping you be the precious element you are, to be poured forth from a clay vessel.

Pray today that you will always remember that you are precious in the eyes of God. Pray today that you will remember the sling and the stone that will slay your Goliath. Pray today that you will be poured forth from a clay vessel in joy and love. Blessings and gentle hugs today, dear friend.

Rejoicing

When they saw the star, they rejoiced with exceedingly great joy.

—Matthew 2:10 (NKJV)

STARS. OH, THEY are a beautiful sight. When was the last time that you were able to just sit outside and look up at a starry night? Twinkly little bursts from here, big bursts from wherever they are. Do you go walking under a starry night holding hands, and sharing all the joy from the day and the stars.

Some seek a long time for the Savior and King. Others find the Savior in the fleeting and passing of a moment. Many watch for a new star for His return, just as the wise men of old watched for His birth. They were the first to truly seek Him, the Savior of the world.

Before He was here, there were those seeking for Him—some with joy, some to destroy, always the same story. Today, some seek to find Him with joy, and some to destroy.

What are you seeking? We have wandered through valleys and trudged up hills. We have met at the edge of cliffs and hung from the steepest of mountaintops. We have had days of tears, days of joy, days of sorrow, and days to rejoice. It is now time to hang onto that rejoicing—rejoicing for the soul.

When we have joy, we need to sing out to the world! When I was the pianist/organist for a small country church, one of my favorite Christmas hymns, "Emmanuel," was just too precious to hold for the few weeks between Thanksgiving and Christmas. I would often include it in my music for the Lord's Supper when we shared it, calling on the name of the Lord, oh, Emmanuel, oh, to love on Him and rejoice!

When we have joy, we need to sing out to the world. Who cares if you can sing? Just open your mouth and sing those beautiful praise songs, Southern gospel songs, traditional hymns, whatever gets you going. We need to sing like the angels from the realms of glory on the first holy night. When we want to rejoice that we have conquered our Goliath, we want to shout it from the mountaintop.

Pray, dear friend, that you will be able to go to the mountaintop often and slay your Goliath over and over, if need be. Pray, dear friend, that you will be able to sing with joy and gladness that you know you are an overcomer of your disease. Your Goliath doesn't hold anything over you, my dear friend! You have come from the pity party to rejoicing all in sixty days. I bid you a fond farewell, my dear friend, with many blessings and gentle hugs.

ABOUT THE AUTHOR

Tami Treat-Boyne grew up in Davenport, Iowa, until her father died. She enjoyed reading and writing her own short stories. After her father passed, she moved to Southwest Missouri, where she can be found today with her loving hubs and her family close by.

Tami was diagnosed in 1997 with fibromyalgia and, in the following years, developed numerous diseases and a plethora of allergies—her Goliath. Through this experience, God has instilled in her a desire to help others fight their Goliaths, walk the valleys, climb the cliffs, travel the trails, and tread the water.

Now Tami writes and goes to speaking events. She prays you will find some humor through each day of your journey and that this book will be a blessing to you as well.

9 798888 436157